# FAR FROM THE TREE

*May You Always
See The Beauty
Inside,
God Bless,
Shari*

# Far From the Tree

SHARI SULLIVAN-QUINN

TATE PUBLISHING
AND ENTERPRISES, LLC

*Far From The Tree*
Copyright © 2014 by Shari Sullivan-Quinn. All rights reserved.

No part of this publication may be reproduced, stored in a retrieval system or transmitted in any way by any means, electronic, mechanical, photocopy, recording or otherwise without the prior permission of the author except as provided by USA copyright law.

This book is designed to provide accurate and authoritative information with regard to the subject matter covered. This information is given with the understanding that neither the author nor Tate Publishing, LLC is engaged in rendering legal, professional advice. Since the details of your situation are fact dependent, you should additionally seek the services of a competent professional.

The opinions expressed by the author are not necessarily those of Tate Publishing, LLC.

Published by Tate Publishing & Enterprises, LLC
127 E. Trade Center Terrace | Mustang, Oklahoma 73064 USA
1.888.361.9473 | www.tatepublishing.com

Tate Publishing is committed to excellence in the publishing industry. The company reflects the philosophy established by the founders, based on Psalm 68:11,
*"The Lord gave the word and great was the company of those who published it."*

Book design copyright © 2014 by Tate Publishing, LLC. All rights reserved.
*Cover design by Nikolai Purpura*
*Interior design by Mary Jean Archival*

Published in the United States of America

ISBN: 978-1-63063-189-5
Biography & Autobiography / Personal Memoirs
14.02.20

Dedicated to My Twin, who
believed in me
Long before I believed
in myself
"Tell me more"

# THE FIRST STEP

*As I look back over the years of my past, I see them unfold as spirals winding back into infinity. In some years the seasons blend rapidly, the coils fitted snugly, one upon the other, like a tightly wound spring; while in other years the coils stretch widely and flow loosely, one onto the next, like a ribbon just fallen from someone's hair. This marks the slowness with which they passed, for they are the years filled with sorrow and sadness, when time itself seemed to stand still and all the world moved around me, while I merely existed inside of myself. A shell performing a daily routine so ingrained, so much a habit, that the only thing that really stands out in my memories of this time is the loneliness, the sadness of the empty ache inside.*

*Moving back along my ribbon of memories, I reach a time when gaps begin to appear, spaces of emptiness along the spirals. At first they are only short gaps marking small sections of time, but the farther back I travel the larger the gaps, until entire seasons unfold with nothing to mark their passing. And while I know that I lived and that I was during those times, there are no memories to give acknowledgment of my existence. I cannot help but wonder what is perhaps stored in my subconscious of this time.*

*The strongest memories call out to me, those of birthdays and holidays, the days of my children's births. There are, of course, also* special memories that I pause to linger over—my wedding day, my graduation, even the day that I at last received my driver's license. Then there are the private memories such as my first kiss or the first time I felt true sexual excitement, the fear and embarrassment associated with my first period, which is such a bittersweet time for a young girl. All the seasons of my past, the waterfall and sunshine that have produced the garden of my life; where has it all gone? All of the dreams and plans so carefully made, and then somewhere among life's daily toils, so easily forgotten, mislaid like a pair of glasses, lost in life's daily shuffle.

I was always going to be and do something important. I grew up as women came of age and I believed there was nothing I could not do or be or conquer. I learned to be outspoken and that a woman did not have to be subservient to a man or pretend to be less intelligent in order to win a provider; they could be the provider, could be equal. However, I was looking for a utopian world—a world where men saw women for their abilities and their intelligence and not just their bodies. Where women stood united and didn't base their own self-worth on looks alone. I was also foolish enough to believe that true love existed and that love based on mutual respect and common interests could withstand the tests of time.

How naïve I was! I didn't realize what a truly large role sex plays in the real world, selling everything from a movie ticket to beer and automobiles. Nor had I any idea how hard a woman must work to be judged for whom she is and what she is capable of, instead of on whether she's built like a Barbie doll. I thought by speaking my mind I was showing my equality; instead, I have been labeled with titles like opinionated, bossy, and even bitch! So, somehow, in spite of all of my ideals, my determination, my certainty of success, I never became anyone or anything but myself.

> Footfalls echo in the memory, down the passage which we did not take, towards the door we never opened, into the rose garden...
>
> —T. S. Eliot

*Life is a matter of choices, of left and right turns. A journey for which there is no map and the clues given are subtle warnings that are seldom heeded. Most think their lives will be somehow different from those that came before, so patterns are repeated over and over again, like the pattern woven into a bolt of fabric, repetitiously, again and again. The threads may be of a different color, the texture slightly changed, but the pattern is the same.*

*I sometimes wonder what might have been had my choices been different, but I never allow the thoughts to linger for a wise man once said, "Be careful what you wish for." So I silently cross myself to ward off evil, for I would never trade parenthood and my three babies for any path not taken, nor any door unopened. But in that brief moment that I do allow these thoughts to pass through my mind, I wonder if it wouldn't have been wiser to have earned a degree before learning about diaper rash and baby shots, Little League and Girl Scout cookie sales, teacher conferences and Christmas pageants. Would that have made me a better parent? Probably not, but maybe it would have given me more confidence to have learned about me before I relinquished my identity to become a mommy.*

*Motherhood is all consuming. You surrender your own wants and needs to contend with the totally selfish demands of an infant and lose yourself in caring for this tiny person who is solely dependent upon you. I recall one of my first lonely 2:00 a.m. feedings as I looked down into the tiny face of my newborn. I was suddenly overwhelmed at the awesome, eternal responsibility of parenthood! A feeling of desperation washed over me as I had never felt before as I truly realized, for the first time, what nine months of pregnancy had not prepared me for—parenting is forever! Unlike anything else we choose to do in life, it truly is forever.*

*When we marry, we promise to love, honor, and cherish until death do us part, but as so many of us know, there are ways out of that. But you can't divorce yourself from parenthood or decide to drop out because it's not for you after all. Oh, I know there's always adoption, but somehow I feel that once a mother has looked upon a tiny newborn's face, or felt the thrusts of tiny limbs within her womb, motherhood is with her forever. Somewhere deep inside you change, and even if someone else raises the child, you always know that somewhere out there is a speck of humanity, a breath of life that you are responsible for creating. Creation, what a wondrous, overwhelming, marvelous thing! So simplistically beautiful that we take it for granted, and yet it is so awesomely miraculous!*

*So yes, parenthood is forever, beyond the terrible twos and the first day of school. Beyond prom night and driver's education, beyond the birth of your first grandchild even, you are always the parent, the elder generation. It spirals off into the future, the unknown, just as the past spirals back into the darkness, to the beginning. Each generation, each parent and child, a part of the one that came before, merging, blending one into the other; flowing backward into the sea of faces, of humanity, all a part of the great sea of life. While we may search eternally for the meaning of life, still we procreate. For in spite of our knowledge, our ability to splice genes and toy with genetics, to send rockets soaring into space and satellites to photograph other planets, we are still driven by instinct and hormones, by the age-old need to blend those genes into new life and thus somehow feel we have gained a bit of eternity.*

*I have never believed that anyone is a "natural born parent" but I suppose for some, it comes easier than for others. But like learning the self-control to stop a bad habit, it comes with time and effort. I truly love being a mother but I won't say it came easily. I was very intimidated by my first newborn. I read manuals and studied books and asked for advice wherever I could find it, weeding through the information to find the truly helpful tidbits. It took awhile for me to realize that there is no one right way; in the end we must choose the way that seems best to us, what feels right, the most natural for us.*

*Over the years I have been a mother lion protecting her cubs, feeling their hurts and their slights, their sadness and successes as deeply as my own. Gradually, painfully, I have started to let go, to allow them to fight their own battles, to make their own choices. It hasn't been easy. As I watch them grow through their adolescent years and beyond, I realize how dependent I have become on their need of me and how lost I feel without them. For nearly twenty years, all of my struggles have always been to give them happy memories of childhood and somewhere in the struggle, I have lost myself. I have forgotten what it means to be anyone except Mommy.*

*When I think about it, I realized that for the past several years, both before and after my divorce from Billy, in the good times and the bad, it has been as if I held my breath…waiting…just waiting… but for what? For something wondrous and magical to lift me up, to rescue me, ease my burden, ease the weight of the struggle, to take care of me and change my life into all that I had dreamed it would ever be? Sadly, I have to face the dawn and remind myself that there are no knights on white horses, no heroes to come and save a dreamer like me.*

*Whoever I am, whatever I have or have not become, rests solely on my shoulders. If fulfillment or contentment has escaped me then perhaps it is because there is an emptiness inside of me, a void that only I can fill. Without clearly understanding who I am, how I became this person and what caused this void, it seems there is no way to go forward. So I have decided to go back, into my past, and discover what has shaped this person I call self. You little book, are to be my time machine. I once read that a journal is a good form of self-healing, and oh how I need to be healed! There is an ache inside of me, a tenderness that won't go away. I have kept diaries and journals off and on over the years, but they were always of the present; you will be a combination of past and present—just like me. Perhaps together we can find the little girl again and try to recapture the dreams she cherished.*

*The words of a remembered song, slip through my mind, "Buy me a ticket on the last train out tonight." I can hear the wheels of the train clickity-clack; clickity-clack going round and round inside of my head until the sounds blend to become the ticking of a clock, marking the passage of time and I think, time passes, is passing, every moment, of every day. And I realize that whether we choose to take the necessary steps to reach our goals or we sit back and wait for rescue, it will continue to pass, for time waits for no man or woman. Each season will continue to merge with the next, as gently, as surely as a river flows to the sea; this great river of life that flows into the sea of humanity. And whether we choose to ride the rapids or stay in the shallows, it flows ever forward carrying us along, however reluctantly.*

# A Thousand Miles

Tess sighed as she closed the small fabric-covered book that she had been writing in, her hand tracing the floral pattern on its back. She had chosen it because of the pretty old-fashioned look the cloth cover gave. It looked like the sort of book a lady would choose to keep her journal in and she loved the faded yellow tint of the pages, just waiting for her pen to stroke them. It reminded her of the diary in the novel *Nineteen Eighty-Four*.

She felt better now that she had taken the first step. It was often said that a journey of a thousand miles began with the first step. Now all she had to do was keep putting one foot in front of the other until she felt whole again—one step at a time. This emptiness inside of her was frightening. It felt as if she'd been carrying the "whole load" of life's responsibilities for so long and she was tired, overwhelmingly tired, bone deep tired. Even before her divorce from Billy six years ago, she had carried the load, but never, ever had she so longed for someone to share the burden as she did now.

The first few years after her separation from Billy had been so filled with adjustment that they had passed very swiftly. The kids had grown from children to teens and she'd been so busy trying to make their lives better, to achieve something for their benefit that time had flown on past. Maybe that was the root of her discontent, for in spite of all of her struggles and her determination, they still could barely make ends meet. As the kids had grown, so had their needs, and while they could work part-time now and meet some of their own expenses, there were still so many things she longed to give them, do for them before it was too late, before they grew up resenting her for all that she had failed to do.

When they were babies, she had envisioned a "typical" middle-class childhood for them, complete with braces and ballet classes, a good safe dependable car when they were old enough to drive, college educations after high school, and most of all, a father who would care about these things as well. Sadly, reality was far removed from her visions.

They seldom heard from Billy. His child support had been sporadic over the years, and it took all that she earned just to feed them and keep a roof over their heads. Sometimes she swore her old car ran on prayer, and if not for Grant letting Chad drive one of the farm trucks, he wouldn't have a vehicle at all. They existed paycheck to paycheck and she prayed each night that they all stayed healthy so that there would be no overwhelming medical bills to face.

It had been so long since they'd enjoyed a family dinner out, other than fast-food occasionally, and she couldn't remember the last time she'd bought a new outfit for herself. Her clothes were usually hand-me-downs from her sister Becca, or from Patty, Uncle Grant's wife. Tressa and Chad bought most of their own clothes now, but whenever she did have anything extra to spend, it always went to meet their needs first. Now their childhood years were almost over, it was nearly too late—she had failed.

When she and Billy had first separated, she had tried dating, hoping to find someone to share her life with, someone to help carry part of life's load, or at least someone who would listen when she talked about her troubles. After several awkward dates ranging from dull to total disasters, she'd given up on the dating scene and refused to agree to anymore blind dates from well-meaning friends. If being single was the good life, then Tess had somehow missed it.

From the stilted conversations of first dates to fending off sexual advances at the end of the evening, there was nothing she enjoyed about casual dating. She didn't believe in one-night stands or in allowing herself to be picked up by a stranger. Somehow it all made her feel like a side of beef in a meat market or a good dependable used car on a lot with shiny new sports cars. She wasn't a knockout, didn't have unusually large breasts or shiny blond hair that cascaded down her back. She didn't know how to play the helpless female game.

She didn't have the money to spend on the things that seemed to attract men: perfect manicures, highlighted hair, caps for her teeth, expensive purses, perfume, sexy high heels and stylish clothing; she was just herself—clean hair, short nails and all. She didn't pretend or play games and couldn't promote herself other than honestly. But men weren't looking for honesty; they wanted sex appeal. She needed friendship before sex; men just wanted sex. She liked sincerity, intimacy on an intellectual level before advancing to intimacy on a physical level; men didn't want intimacy at all—they just wanted hot, uncomplicated sex. She wanted fidelity; a woman shouldn't have to worry about being compared to anyone else when making love with her man. She wanted a committed relationship. She wanted all the words men hated. Men weren't looking for any type of relationship. They didn't want closeness and friendship; they weren't longing for a soul mate; they wanted freedom, variety, the right to bed whomever they wanted whenever they wanted. It had been hard accepting these facts at first, and like so many things in life, it had come through painful experience.

Her old coworker Lisa had recently moved away to Virginia Beach. They had met not long after Tess and Billy had separated.

Though their personalities were complete opposites, Lisa had been very helpful and supportive during the complications of divorce, having just survived one herself. Her vibrant, outgoing manner had helped Tess keep her perspective, and her bawdy sense of humor had lifted many depressive days.

Lisa dated casually, picking up men in bars or online for "recreational" sex, as she called it, and she had shocked Tess with her stories. Tess vehemently refused to join her on her "outings" but listened in astonished amazement at the stories the older woman shared; she confided that about half the men she picked up were married, maybe more, but if they didn't volunteer the information, and many did, she didn't bother asking. Her reasoning was that if it wasn't her, it would be someone else; all men were scum and only good for one thing in Lisa's opinion. Her rationalization was that it was just sex, not love and romance.

After living with Billy, Tess couldn't understand Lisa's casualness. She tried to make her see that somewhere on the other side of that one-night stand was a woman who had no idea she was married to a creep who couldn't keep his fly zipped. Besides, how could she be so casual about something that was anything but? Tess calmly tried to keep her amazement to herself. Lisa on the other hand learned to carefully omit certain bits of information when sharing tales of her outings upon hearing about the younger woman's marriage.

For Tess, sex and intimacy were all tied up together inside and she couldn't imagine one without the other, nor did she want to. She didn't understand how anyone could turn their emotions on and off like that. Sex was so much more than just the physical joining of two bodies, it was the greatest possible way to say "I care," and without the emotion, the caring and the tenderness, it seemed empty and meaningless. It seemed wrong to cheapen something so wonderful by sharing it with just anyone who said yes, no matter how great the physical need. She did not believe any human being was truly programmed that way; it seemed that to do so would reduce one to an animalistic level. No matter how much a person might deceive themselves into believing casual sex was uninvolved, how could you share something so intimate and personal, so filled with pleasure—with the give and take of that pleasure—and not feel a certain amount of tenderness towards them?

Lisa told her that these feelings were just the afterglow of good sex; that guys didn't feel that same tenderness and were willing to have sex with someone they didn't even like as a person if it were offered. It all seemed very cold and calculating to Tess, and she didn't want to waste those feelings of tenderness with someone she barely knew. After all, why have such pleasurable experiences with someone you cared about in only the most basic way any human being cares about another? It all became very empty and meaningless when you looked at it that way, and to Tess, all of life should have meaning. Life without meaning seemed destructive to the soul and that wasn't for her. Some things shouldn't be cheapened; to do so, cheapened life itself.

There had been only once, since her divorce from Billy, that Tess had lowered her guard and allowed a man to get close to her emotionally as well as physically. She had met him at Posterity Studios where she worked as a photographer and a videographer. He had sold her boss, Ross Mathews, some new equipment that included free setup and training. She had worked with Ross for six years at that point and was the assistant manager, so she had sat in on the training.

The process had taken most of the week and the salesman Troy, had worked in the field for many years, so he truly understood the equipment as well as the business they worked in. His training was thorough and complete and Tess was surprised to find she enjoyed working with him. As a rule, she found salesmen to be pushy and arrogant, but Troy was charming and attentive in a positive, nonthreatening way and seemed to admire her intelligence as well as her appearance. It was this that first lowered her guard.

After all, so few men really talked to a woman unless they were working towards the bedroom, so she had been surprised when he sought her opinion and seemed truly interested in what she had to say.

By the end of the training, she had been as comfortable working with him as she was with Ross, so when he asked her to join him for dinner, she hesitated only briefly before accepting. Even though she had criticized herself for her bubble of excitement, she couldn't help but hope she might be at the start of something positive in her life.

They had gone to one of the best restaurants in town, making her nervous and self-conscious as she was very much aware of her old clothes and worn purse. But Troy had soon put her at ease, opening doors and holding her chair, as if she were decked out in the latest fashion, carrying a $500 purse instead of one of Becca's hand-me-downs. He had been attentive during dinner, listening when she talked and asking just the right questions to draw her out, getting her to reveal far more of herself than she intended. His replies to her questions had seemed thoughtful. He shared opinions about life and reaching goals that she had always secretly believed but had never voiced for fear of ridicule, such as following one's heart, and removing negativity and negative people from your life.

They seemed so well suited that even their silence was comfortable and companionable. Soon she found herself accepting a second date. By the third date, she knew she was infatuated. It was scary and exciting all at once, so much so that when he asked her to go away with him for a private weekend, she didn't hesitate. Her longing for intimacy with him had surprised her, as had the eagerness she felt to have his body close to hers.

The sex was even more magical than she had imagined. He had been a skilled lover and she was a more than eager pupil. The intensity of their lovemaking had literally left her breathless and by the end of their two days together, she knew she was in far, far over her head, and in danger of being swept away by emotions she wasn't yet ready to identify.

When she arrived for work on Monday, Ross had teased her about the bounce in her step, and it was true, she felt lighter than air. At lunch time, just as a florist delivered a large bouquet of flowers from Troy, the telephone rang. Smiling at the sweet message on the card attached to the bouquet, she absentmindedly reached for the phone, and then after a brief moment, her happiness had shattered like so much broken glass around her feet.

The caller had identified herself as Troy's wife, and that had said it all. Troy was married and his wife assured her there would be no divorce. Troy was a player and Tess was just the latest in a long string of affairs. "You can keep seeing him until he tires of you if you want, but don't think it's ever going anywhere," she informed Tess before hanging up.

Tess slowly lowered the phone to the cradle before tossing the flowers into the trash. One look at her face and Ross had sent her home for the day, where she'd sat in a bubble bath and cried until there were no more tears and her fingers were wrinkled, the water long since gone cold. How could she have been so stupid? How could she have allowed herself to fall so easily? Her self-confidence had shattered along with her heart; after all, if you couldn't trust yourself, who could you trust?

Troy had called just as darkness arrived and she had silently listened to his pleadings. He had begged her forgiveness, swearing that his marriage was a sham. He told her they were actually separated but his wife refused to let go, refused to agree to a divorce. "Just please, give me some time," he pleaded. "She does this every time I try to move on. Please believe me." But Tess had quietly hung up the phone, and then disconnected it from the wall so he couldn't call back.

He had lied to her, allowed her to believe they were at the start of something, but how could he begin something new when he hadn't yet closed the door on his past? Maybe he was trying, and maybe his wife was preventing him from moving on. If he had been honest from the beginning, she might have been willing to take a chance, but finding out this way had been such a shock, such a betrayal. After Billy—sweet lovable, believable Billy—she just couldn't trust someone who'd lied to her from the start.

He had been persistent at first, calling so frequently she had finally gotten an unlisted phone number. Ross had prevented him from seeing her at the studio the few times he'd tried, and she either returned his gifts and cards unopened or tossed them in the trash, until eventually, after a few weeks went by, he had given up.

Slowly, she had gone forward and put it behind her or at least she was able to pretend that she had recovered; but inside, her confidence was gone while her heart still ached. It would have been better to have never known what she was missing than to taste it knowing it could never be hers. Her heart now ached for closeness, her body too, but no longer trusting her ability to recognize the right person, she closed the door to her heart and soul and filled her life by focusing on her work and her kids.

She spent five days a week at the studio and did outside jobs on the weekends, taping weddings and photographing special events. The extra money was welcome and it left her too busy to miss what she didn't have, or at least it had until recently. But lately, when families came in for portraits or she went to tape a graduation or a wedding and she saw loving couples living in nice homes with all of the trappings, standing proudly with their children, children who were sheltered and loved by both parents, her heart ached. It was hard not to be envious. Why couldn't that be her with her children? Why was it that no man had ever wanted to "take care" of her? She realized this was an antiquated idea. Women could take care of themselves but it would have been nice to have someone to lean on occasionally.

But she tried hard not to dwell on the things she didn't have, so she constantly reminded herself to look for the positive. After all, she had chosen this course. She had opened the door and walked through, and it was too late to go back and walk the path not taken, or change the outcome of her decisions.

"I am at this moment the sum of all my past decisions," Tess whispered to herself. And all that she could do at this point was to continue to move forward. She would find a way to heal the aches, the hurts, and a way to fill the emptiness in her soul; a way to unlock the pain and let it all out until she felt whole again.

# Deja Vu

Tess pushed the release button on the tape compartment of the 8mm camera and waited while the tiny computer brain followed her command. She had just finished taping a children's wear fashion show, and her neck and shoulders ached from standing with her arms in the same position for so long. Much of the footage had been shot handheld with the help of the steady cam; even the small camera could quickly get heavy. The studio owned an excellent tripod complete with dolly, but with children, often the most artistic shots came up close with camera in hand; it looked less intimidating that way and it was possible to get more relaxed, natural shots.

She took her work seriously and tried to tell the entire "story" from her viewfinder. This seriousness combined with her natural creativity made her very good at what she did. The studio had a reputation for good work and was usually booked up weeks in advance. They probably could have doubled their staff and still stayed busy, but both she and Ross liked to keep a high quality level which they both felt required personal attention to every aspect of the product they turned out.

Tess did all of the video camera work and the rough edits, but the credit for the finished product had to go to Ross, who personally did the final edits and assembly, including special effects. They functioned together as a team, and with the use of the high quality equipment Ross purchased for the studio, they produced a first class product.

Tess glanced up from packing the equipment as Ms. Kirkenbaum, the modeling coach who had hired the studio to tape the fashion show, approached. The tapping of her stiletto heels on the tile floor of the mall concourse could be heard even over the din of noise all around them. Tess studied the older woman as she approached. She was a vision of perfection, from her carefully coifed hair to her neatly manicured nails, and the expensive, perfectly tailored suit that she wore. Tess smiled to herself trying to picture Ms. Kirkenbaum looking harried and frumpy as she herself seemed to spend most of her time. It was nice to realize that she'd finally reached a point in her life where she no longer felt intimidated at events like this as she would have only a few years before. She was used to being the only woman in jeans or casual slacks and flats. It hadn't taken her long to realize that people rarely paid attention to the person behind the camera, only to the camera itself, so she was accustomed to being treated as part of the décor or as wait staff.

"How'd it go?" Ms. Kirkenbaum asked when she was within ear shot.

"Really well, I think we have some very nice footage here." Tess smiled at the older woman who appeared to be in her mid to late fifties, but it was hard to tell. The skin of her face was taunt and tight as though it had been lifted, so there were no determining age lines there. The excellent cheekbones which made her features striking were genetic and it was evident that while Clarrisa Kirkenbaum was still a very attractive woman, she had been a beauty in her youth.

"Were you able to get good close ups of the boys? I don't usually get many boys to work a fashion show and I want some footage to use for portfolios for advertising work." Ms. Kirkenbaum held herself regally, her posture picture perfect.

Tess felt the need to stand straighter herself as she replied to the other woman, vaguely wondering if she too had modeled before becoming a coach. *Every life has a story*, she thought with a smile, *everyone is a compilation of all that came before*. She assured the older woman that she had indeed gotten good close ups of the five boys that had modeled in the show as she briefly thought about life's path and how lives could be similar, but each was unique to the individual actually living it.

Hitting the replay button on the camera, she held it out for Ms. Kirkenbaum to review. As she showed the other woman the controls, her mind wondered, remembering the old saying, *Nothing new under the sun*, which was so true. Even the abstract thought patterns that flitted through one's mind were not new. Someone at some time probably had similar thoughts for not even an inventors' creation was theirs alone; it was usually based on work that had come before or built from ideas someone else had put down.

Mentally giving herself a shake, she apologized to Ms. Kirkenbaum, "I'm sorry, what did you ask?"

"How long before I can view a final copy?" the other woman repeated patiently. She was used to dealing with children so she had a great deal of patience.

But Tess was embarrassed to be caught wool gathering and she blushed slightly as she replied, "It will probably take a week or so, but we'll give you a call as soon as we know for sure. I'm not sure what Ross's schedule is like, but I'll get to the rough edits as soon as possible."

"That's fine, I'm just anxious—" Ms. Kirkenbaum stopped talking suddenly, smiling at someone behind Tess. "Have you met my son?" she asked.

Tess shook her head and turned to look up at the tall handsome man that had somehow approached without her noticing. He looked to be nearing forty, which would probably make his mother a little older than she'd thought. He had his mother's cheekbones and carried himself with the same poise and she briefly wondered if he too had modeled or if he'd just had lots of instruction from his mother. Remembering her manners, she wiped her hand on her jeans before reaching it out to grasp the hand that he offered. "Tess Quinlan," she told him as his hand closed over hers.

"Bob Kirkenbaum." He smiled, revealing perfect teeth and a dimple in his left cheek. "Mother has shown me some of your previous work. I'm impressed."

Tess returned his smile. "Thank you for your compliment, but most of the credit goes to Ross. He does the final edits and the assembly. I'm just the camera…person."

Bob grinned noting her slight pause before using the *politically correct* term. His eyes quickly taking in her slender figure and petite build. "You're right; you are definitely not a cameraman. But don't discredit what you do. All the editing in the world can't make something from nothing. The shots have to be there first in order to be edited in."

Tess smiled again. She wasn't discrediting her work, just stating a fact. Shooting footage was easy and she enjoyed it—it hardly seemed like work at all except for the ache in her shoulders. It was the frustrating hours in front of the editing equipment that brought forth the polished results that the customers saw, but now hardly seemed the time to argue her point. "Well, thank you for your vote of confidence. I enjoy my work." She bent down to the camera case and pulled out a business card and handed it to him. "If you ever need our services, give us a call. Gina handles the appointments. She's our office 'gofer' and works the front counter, although I think she prefers the term 'girl Friday!'" She smiled. "She handles the scheduling and can get you set up."

He took the card slowly from her hand with a look of surprise on his face. "Ross is a lucky man having a dedicated employee like you. He better hope you never go into business for yourself. You could give him some real competition."

Tess forced a smile. "Thank you." She wished they would move on and leave her to her packing. She hated small talk and his words had struck a nerve, giving her a feeling of déjà vu. Ross often told her the same thing—that he'd be in trouble if she went into business for herself. What neither man seemed to realize was that she just wasn't that brave yet. Her shoulders were carrying about as much responsibility as she could handle right now. She didn't need to add such a major thing as running her own business.

Bob and his mother turned to greet some of the parents, so she quickly turned back to her packing. The parents would want copies of some of the footage as well so her four hours of taping would bring a lot of profit for the studio. Thinking of Ross's favorite saying, "Nothing happens until the sale is made" brought a smile to her face and relieved some of the tension from her shoulders.

As she packed, Bob watched her, noting how she carefully rolled the cords and tucked each piece into the slotted carrying case. Most people would have just tossed everything helter-skelter into the case, but as tired as she must be, she was still taking the time to put everything in its proper place. He smiled and felt his admiration for her growing as he remembered the way she had tossed his mild flirtation back into his face by handing him a business card and instructing him to call her "girl Friday" for an appointment. Here she was, all five feet nothing of her, dressed more for a day in the park while the women around her were dressed to the nines, but she was still so filled with self-confidence that when a man gave her a compliment, she brushed him off with the equivalent of "don't call us, we'll call you." She reminded him of a feisty terrier, not big as a minute but very determined. He wondered what had made her so cautious even while thinking what a formidable business partner she would make. Tucking the thought into his mind for another day, he glanced at Tess one last time before turning back to his mother.

# APPLES AND ORANGES

October 23

Memories are like jewelry. The most precious we keep carefully stored and only bring out on special occasions; but most are costume pieces, things we carry with us daily and never give much thought to. And then of course, there are those that we wish we could discard but can never bring ourselves to. These are the painful pieces, the ones kept wrapped in gauze and safely tucked away at the bottom of our jewelry box—that special ring from an old boyfriend, the last pin our mother's gave us before passing; things that make us a little sad. We rarely take these pieces out and when we do, it's usually in private, reflective moments when we can slowly unwrap them and look upon them unobserved.

I found my first gray hair today, a startling moment in a woman's life, but not as depressing as first discovering the tiny lines around one's eyes. Grow old with grace and dignity—that is my goal. But do I want to grow old alone? My children will develop their own lives, make their own homes; they aren't mine to keep forever, I have only been allowed to care for them until they can care for themselves. Then what? Lisa says no one wants to be alone, but I'm not sure it matters. After all, aren't we all eternally alone inside of ourselves anyway? No matter how much you love someone, you can't actually be a part of them. We all bear this aching aloneness as if we have lost our way home. Perhaps that is what life is all about; perhaps it is a searching, a journey to find our way home again, back to the place we were before we were born; back to the memories we lost at the moment of birth.

So now my therapy begins, but where do I start? At the beginning? Or with whatever comes to mind? There are so many thoughts flickering inside of me as fireflies trapped inside a glass jar, each crying, "Look at me!" So it seems impossible to choose where to begin.

"Once upon a time in a land far, far away, there lived a little girl. She grew up knowing that she was *special* and that life held only good things for her. But then one day, the grotesque monster called *reality* reared his ugly head and proclaimed her his prisoner. Sadly, she discovered there are no keys to open the door to the magic kingdom called life."

There's a saying that goes something like "a bad apple never falls far from the tree." When I was a young girl, I hated that saying. I wanted to fall far, far from the tree. And I truly believed I could—I believed if a person only worked hard enough they could be anything they wanted to be. But being something or becoming something is easy, like playing a part on a stage. I have *been* many things in my life—a mother, a waitress, a videographer, a good little girl, but they were all just roles, parts that I have played. Deep inside, nothing has changed. I am still just me, the person my genes and my environment programmed me to be. There is no escape through *being* something.

To truly change we must change what's inside, change how we see ourselves or at least its effect on us; after all, if an apple fell into an orange grove, it would still be an apple. No matter how much it might admire the bright, fragrant oranges, it would always be an apple. So no matter what role I play, nothing will change until I first change the picture inside, otherwise, I will always be what my reflexes guide me to be, what my inner self sees and has always seen, *the child of an alcoholic.*

Children of alcoholics often become alcoholics themselves or abusers of other substances. They also tend to marry alcoholics or other dependent personality types, seeking perhaps to cure the parent they could not save. Others become overachievers and workaholics, in an attempt to feel equal to their peers for they see themselves as less, not as good as or beneath others. And still others live up to this low image of themselves by not being able to hold a job or to deal with the stress of day-to-day living; they drift aimlessly through life always looking for rescue. Even if they are never substance abusers themselves, their own children are still prone to these same pitfalls, somehow having inherited the alcoholic tendencies. Escape from the cycle is very hard, and abuse can often be traced back for generation after generation after generation.

For most of my life I have denied the existence of these scars and pretended that I had escaped unscathed, but I know that this isn't true. After all, I married Billy. I know that the scars are with me and they have dictated my steps even while I refused to acknowledge them. Now I must bring the shadows into the light, examine them, analyze them, and find a way to get beyond the fear and the pain.

Journey

Windowpanes with fingerprints
Mar a perfect view.
Ashtrays with cigarettes,
Tell me what to do!
Time an endless carousel
Turning all the same.
Life, the soul's carnival,
How'd you play this game?
Me, I'm just a poor dreamer,

Dream my life away.
Done with smoke and mirrors,
All illusions anyway.
The grass is always greener,
Flowers, never weeds.
My yard, it's much meaner,
Flowers gone to seeds.
Whatever song is playing,
However old the tune,
Me, I'll not be saying
Words to fit the mood.
Always out of sync and step,
Marching somehow wrong.
A path I haven't found yet,
A heart that beats as strong.
But somehow I will find it,
Without map or clue.
And I'll complete this journey
And give this life it's due!!

—S. Smith

Tess slowly rose and stretched her arms over her head. Her back and shoulders still ached after the long hours of taping and even the hot bath hadn't helped much. Retrieving her journal, she checked the fire in the woodstove and headed down the hallway to her room, pausing first to look in on Tressa as she slept.

Tressa was fifteen going on twenty-five and she made Tess feel ancient. She had been so thrilled to have a daughter, but now she sometimes wondered if they would ever be close. Tressa had been independent and rebellious even as a toddler, getting into more scrapes and mischief than either of the boys had. She was still stubborn and independent and everything became a battle between them, from the amount of makeup she wore to not being allowed to car date, she fought against every rule.

Tess gently smoothed the mass of dark brown curls from her face and bent to kiss her cheek, something Tressa didn't allow when she was awake. She'd been premature and had spent several weeks in an incubator when they weren't allowed to hold her. Tess had often wondered if this absence of physical contact had left her with her aversion to hugs and physical displays of affection. Her daughter was a beauty and she dreaded the next few years. Holding her back was going to prove a real challenge.

Moving on to the boy's room, she pulled the covers over Sammy, her youngest, and kissed his freckled nose. Sammy was everyone's baby and even at his most mischievous he was the "good one." He never tried to hurt her and to always be pleasing. This desire to please probably came from being the youngest. She could remember feeling the same way as a child; that she needed somehow to compensate for the mistakes of her older siblings.

Chad, her oldest, was seventeen and at just over six feet tall, he overflowed the bunk beds that he and Sammy shared. In spite of his size, he was just an overgrown little boy to her. She worried about his future; he would be graduating in the spring but he still seemed unfocused and refused to discuss college or education beyond high school. He had worked at Pizza Hut for over a year now and talked often of becoming a manager, but Tess couldn't see a future in pizza, so she worried. But maybe she was just pushing him to be something instead of waiting to see who he already was.

Uncle Grant had told her that Chad just lacked motivation, and together they had tried to instill it in him. Grant ran the small farm where her house sat, plus he owned an accounting business that provided a range of clerical services to other businesses. He was moderately successful and had tried to interest Chad in some aspect of his business. Chad had been amiable but had stated he preferred dealing with the public when they were relaxed and hungry, and not stressing over the IRS. Besides, he found accounting boring and he couldn't see doing a job he didn't like just to make a lot of money. Tess could see his point. She was very thankful she found her own job fun and rewarding, but she had hoped he would show a sincere interest in working with Grant.

His bosses at the restaurant really liked him and he had already been promoted to assistant weekend shift manager, which was an accomplishment for someone so young. But pizza maker had never entered her fantasies when she thought of her son's future. She blamed herself for allowing him to grow up with no positive male role model. She should have been more understanding of his needs. She should have tried to help him become more focused when he was younger, something—anything! Surely she could have directed him and done more than she had, which was just to tell herself that it would all work out, that he would grow up someday and find his place.

Now time was running out and she worried that he would end up like his dad, drifting from job to job with no real direction in his life. It seemed all she could do now was to be supportive and pray. Surely if God could move mountains, he could move 180 pound boys like Chad.

# My Many Daddies

October 24

When I was still very young, maybe five or six years old, I remember asking my mom about a memory that often haunted me, just an image really, that would flash into my mind and leave me feeling fearful and tense. It was an image of children being beaten. I had always thought that one of the children must have been me but I had suddenly come to realize that they were all older and larger than I was even at that time, so it was impossible that the beating had actually occurred to me. I had always been told that I had scarcely been spanked, nothing more than a swat or two on the rear. Since there were no words with this "memory" I decided that it must have been a vivid dream that left fragmented images stored in my subconscious.

As I grew older, I learned that it is possible to have memories from infancy, from a time when we have no words and no concept of language to go with the images and impressions stored inside. My mother had assured me that the memory couldn't have been of me, but it still haunted me. After overcoming the fear the image always invoked, I studied it carefully and gradually remembered many details that told me who and what it was.

At the harsh angry words, the baby abruptly stopped crawling and sat on the hardwood floor. Her tiny hands clutched nervously at the cloth diaper she wore as she stared, transfixed, at the image before her—small bodies, those of her siblings, twisted and squirmed, crying, pleading for mercy from the man who struck them with a large leather strap that left angry red welts on their tender flesh. The baby didn't know their words but she recognized their distress, their tears. The man was her father and he cursed at the children, demanding they be still as he beat them with the strap.

The only light in the room came from a bare bulb hanging overhead so their images were distorted and created large, grotesque shadows on the wall. Frightened, the baby urinated. As the warm wetness ran down her legs, it was quickly chilled by the cool draft of air blowing under the door. The baby shivered, partially from the cold but also from fear. The urge to "get away" was strong, overwhelming, but yet she sat, paralyzed by her fear.

Her father continued to deal out blows until the children had no more strength to cry and he was too tired to continue. As his hand grew still at last, he seemed to feel her eyes upon him, and he turned quickly to look at her. Returning his stare, she held her breath as her pulse pounded in her ears. She could sense the heightened excitement that radiated from him, and it sickened her even as an infant; she knew her father had enjoyed this brutal display of domination. Her fear of him cried out inside of her, and yet she could not move and could not crawl away. Gasping suddenly for air, her breathing quickened. This was Daddy, one of her caretakers, and yet in that moment she hated him.

*Get away, must get away!* The message flashed repeatedly in her mind; her breathing becoming more and more labored as she found herself unable to break his gaze, overwhelmed by her loathing and her fear of him. Her chest tightened and began a wheezing sound as the tightness and the shortness of breath turned to a full blown asthma attack. She cringed away from him as he reached to pick her up, unable to cry out or make a sound. The wheezing quickened as she angled away from his touch. She tried to slow her breathing because even as a baby, she knew that anything could annoy him, could bring down his wrath.

Suddenly, the door opened, bringing a wash of cold air into the room. It was her uncle and her momma, home at last. *Mommy!* she thought, but it was her Uncle Grant that scooped her from her father's arms. He quickly assessed the situation, sparing an understanding glance for her siblings who were now quietly huddled together on the old worn sofa, their tear stained faces silent and their small hands quietly rubbing the red welts that were rising on their skin. She could feel the tension in his hands as he handed her to her mother. Her father looked at him, a look filled with contempt and challenge, but Grant was still little more than a boy with the scrawniness of adolescence still upon him, and his brother was strong from long hours of shoveling coal.

When Grant at last looked away, her father turned to her mother and demanded, "Get her medicine so she'll stop that infernal noise and then get in there and make some supper."

*My heart goes out to the baby I was then, for in that moment I lost my innocence and learned to fear one of the very people that circumstances forced me to rely on for my very existence. Even now, as I recall that memory, I can see no remorse on my father's face, no pain in punishing his children; just that sense of excitement, of enjoyment. I think his domination of his family made him feel powerful; it gave him control, absolute control, as he forced them to bend to his will.*

*I think I must have decided at that exact moment to always be very, very good so that he would never strike me like that. Yet even while I feared him, I loved him. He was my daddy, and there were many daddies in the man that was my father. One was this cruel tyrant who* beat my siblings, but another was the man that—as I grew older—would leave treats for me to find at the bottom of his coal dust covered lunch box. When he arrived home from work, he would hold his hands out for me to run and give him a hug and then he would hand over the lunchbox. Sometimes the treat would be a Little Debbie cake or a piece of spearmint chewing gum—treats that we didn't ordinarily get, treats that were bought only for his lunch.

He was the daddy who would clap his hands and encourage me to do the twist as my brother strummed his old guitar, who took me fishing when I was five, and with a gnarled stick called a "jerk pole," helped me to catch my first fish. But in the nine short years of my life until his death, I never lost my fear of him. I always tried hard to be pleasing, to be a good little girl, to never cross him or invoke his anger.

I escaped his punishment, not because I was so good, but because my siblings carefully kept me out of his way when he was angry or when I had broken something or disobeyed one of his many rules. But also possibly because by the time I came along, his drinking had overtaken him to the point that he spent much of my childhood either sick or in the hospital or in a drunken stupor, no longer able to beat anyone or even to care for his own self.

His alcoholism was something that we all learned very early not to discuss, not with anyone. Not our neighbors or friends, not our relatives, not even among ourselves. It was easier to pretend it wasn't really all that bad than to face the truth. Also, in those days, there was shame associated with alcoholism not just for the alcoholic, but also for the entire family, as if we too had some weaknesses about us because he couldn't control his drink. This lesson came so early in my life that I have no recollection of learning it; it was simply the way things were. We didn't discuss it because it meant facing the shameful truth.

There was a small creek that ran behind our house and, in those days, any trash that couldn't be burned, fed to the various farm animals, or added to the compost was disposed of by tossing it into the creek. That sounds pretty appalling in today's world of environmental concerns, but this was years before people started becoming concerned with mankind's excesses. Another thing that we didn't discuss was that on the sloping hillside from our backyard down to the creek, there was a virtual truckload of beer cans. Enough cans that if we could have turned them into bricks we could have lived in a fine brick house, twice the size of our own. And when the spring rains came and the creek flooded its banks, the cans would be washed away as if they had never been.

There were other things we didn't discuss, like why he laid for days at a time on the living room couch, not going to work, not coming to the table for meals, only rising to urinate and ask for more to drink. Or the nights we cringed in fear in our beds when he would beg and plead with Mom to give him money or to make Grant get out of bed to drive him to buy more beer. We would huddle together as his drunken yell filled the air echoed by Mom's soft voice and the occasional slap of his hand against her flesh. We huddled together for comfort, but still we didn't discuss it.

The lessons of pretending were so ingrained that for years I have pushed away the bad memories and continued the pretense, telling myself that those times were infrequent and it really hadn't been that bad. But the truth is that we all lived under the shadow of fear that he created, both with his drinking and his anger, never knowing when or where his fury would strike, but always hoping that when it was unleashed it wouldn't be directed at us. My siblings were unable to even forge a bond against him because even though it might hurt to watch your sibling get beaten, at least it wasn't you this time, not this time. Anything could set off his fury and you never knew what that thing might be. Something that he would laugh at one day could bring down his wrath the next. It was the uncertainty, the feeling of being always on alert that created the constant tension in our home and that trained me from an early age to be very self aware.

There were some good times, but they were overshadowed by the tension, by the darker times and the fear and uncertainty was woven through the good times so they became only a pretense. "If we don't act like we're having a good time, he'll never bring us again." "We better pretend we like this TV show or he won't let us watch at all tomorrow." Our laughter would be forced and just a little too loud, our efforts halfhearted as we waited for his abuse at our imagined *transgressions. We quickly learned the rules of the make believe games we tried to play to pacify his anger.*

*I realize now with an adult's perspective that my father was just a man, with a man's faults, a man's failures and needs, not the monster he sometimes seemed in my youth. As children, we idolize our parents and make them larger than life, their shortcomings we base on our own failures. "If I were a better kid, he wouldn't have to discipline me." So we fail to see them as merely physical beings who are finding their way in life as best they can. We expect perfection of them; we make them God-like. But now, I see that my father had the needs and dreams of a complex personality, as we all do. His life had been hard, filled with things that left him tense, frustrated and out of control.*

*After witnessing the horrors of WWII, I am sure he needed professional help to deal with the sense of being out of control—of having no control. But in those days, it wasn't chic to see a shrink, it was taboo and the entire neighborhood shunned you. So his way of dealing with these uncontrollable forces inside him was to strike out at his wife and children. If he couldn't control everything in his life, at least he could force his family to march to the beat of his particular drum.*

*During the war, he served under General Patton in Europe and was in five of the major battles including the Invasion of Normandy and the Battle of the Bulge. I remember seeing him cry when he was drunk as he talked about the war. He spoke of an escaping prisoner he'd been forced to shoot in the back, and of the horrors of Normandy beach where bodies fell in your path and you were forced to run over them in an attempt to save your own life; of seeing buddies blown apart at his side and body parts hanging from trees; horrors that only another battle worn soldier would understand. Images that most have never seen and would never want to see. I know these horrors helped to create the harsh, cruel man that he came to be.*

*He was the oldest of my grandmother's eleven children. My grandfather had been married before and had sired seven children by his first wife—three sons and four daughters. When he married* my grandmother, some of these children were already married with children of their own, but the youngest was barely school age. When his first wife had died, he had quickly married my grandmother who was only sixteen. He was thirty years her senior and they married from mutual need, not from any feelings of love. He needed a mother and homemaker for his children, and she had been recently orphaned and was living with an older brother whose wife didn't like having her around, so she needed a home of her own.

As the oldest of my grandmother's children, my father always had to work hard around the farm. Grandpa was nearly fifty when he was born so by the time my father was a pre-teen, most of the farming work was his responsibility. At sixteen, he had gone to work in the coal mines to help pay the taxes on the farm and buy cloth for clothing for the younger children, who were still coming. The youngest, my Uncle Grant, was born shortly after grandpa's seventieth birthday.

There was a five-year gap between my dad and his next closest sibling, and he always felt his mother loved her second child more than she loved him. Grandma, on the other hand, confided to my mother that my dad had been very willful even as a little boy, so that it had been hard to cuddle him or show affection. And maybe Grandma just never had a chance to bond with her first child. Much of my dad's early care was delegated to his older half sisters while grandma tended to the farm and the duties of caring for a large, expanding family. His sisters treated him like a baby doll and constantly carried him and fussed over him, so maybe she was actually jealous of the closeness he seemed to share with his sisters and he mistook her jealousy for a lack of love.

I've often thought that being not yet twenty when Daddy was born, Grandma may have felt inadequate as a mother. With her own mother gone, she had no one to turn to for guidance. Possibly by the time my Uncle Jesse came along, she had grown up somewhat and felt more confident as a parent. Also, by then, the farm that had been in disrepair when she first married my grandfather was back to a productive state and the smoke house and food pantry were once again full, so she had more time to spend with her baby.

*Whatever the reasons for her distance from him as a child, Daddy always felt the need to try and please her as a way of gaining her love. But no matter how much she loved him as an adult, it couldn't seem to make up for the slights he had felt as a child.*

*She taught him to make moonshine when he was barely in his teens, having learned the art from her brothers. Grandpa was getting too old to work in the mines by this time so they sold crops to pay for most of the things that took cash money, but a run of 'shine could raise cash quicker, and with their own corn crops, it was cheaper to make. Grandma was a fussy, no-nonsense type of woman. She kept a neat, organized home and wasted nothing. She taught Daddy to make the 'shine in the same way; she wanted it clean and pure, and tolerated none of the shortcuts some moonshiners took. She never drank it herself and yet she could tell by the smell alone when a batch of fermenting hops was right for "running off."*

*Grandpa always kept some on hand for his morning hot toddy and for purely medicinal purposes, but he never really drank either. Daddy's weakness for it can be traced to his own great-grandfather—paternal side—who died when Daddy was eight years old. As one of the first settlers in the county, it was said that as a young man daddy's great-grandfather had been a drinker and a hell raiser. And in spite of having a wife and several children when he arrived in the county, he didn't settle down and quit drinking until he was in his mid-forties. Of course, by the time Daddy reached his mid-forties it was too late, the alcohol had already done its damage. Daddy died at forty-eight.*

# THE GHOST OF CHRISTMAS

Tess slowly re-read what she had written. It was sketchy but it was a start. Shivering, she rose to add more wood to the woodstove. The nights had grown colder and soon the holiday season would arrive. When she and Billy had first separated, the holidays had depressed her. The first few Christmas mornings, she had felt that if she could just look up and share the children's excitement with another adult, her life would be complete. The feelings had weakened her resolve and made her wonder if maybe they couldn't try again. Then she remembered all those Christmas mornings when he had allowed the children to thank him so sweetly for presents that she had scrimped and saved for. She remembered all the credit he had taken for toys that he had known nothing about until they had been opened as well as surprises that she had thought up and instituted that he would pretend were his ideas.

To Billy, the holidays had just been a good excuse for drinking even more than usual. If he had memories of shared Christmas celebrations, they were shrouded in an alcoholic fog, but maybe he liked it that way, maybe that's what Christmas was all about for him; but not for her, and certainly, not for her children, not anymore. The memories assured her that her decision to leave had been the right one.

Now, in her new life, the holidays were an even busier time than ever, both personally and professionally. The kids were always involved in a variety of activities and the entire month of December was usually filled with pageants and parties, plays and Christmas concerts. Business at the studio always boomed as well as people rushed to get holiday portraits or scheduled tapings of their family get-together or their children's holiday galas. Instead of feeling lonely, she focused her energy on enjoying all the love and gaiety around her. People were so much nicer during the holidays and a warm glow seemed to fill the air. She loved all of it, from the rushing about in the crisp air to the twinkling lights and festive decorations.

The only downside was that there never seemed to be enough time to get it all done; and the shopping of course. She hated Christmas shopping. Crowded store aisles were the one place she found the holiday spirit to be lacking. Harried shoppers become rude as they panicked, worrying that they weren't going to find that perfect gift, so they bumped and grabbed and jostled for positions in overcrowded checkout lines. Ugh! She definitely hated it. Maybe this year, she would get a head start and finish early. The thought made her smile for no matter how positive her intentions, she knew she'd still be out there on Christmas Eve for that one last thing she'd forgotten.

Christmases as a child had been filled with food, from bushel baskets of walnuts and apples, to crates of oranges and boxes of peppermint sticks. The house had been filled with the fragrant aromas and the cheery warmth that came from the old pot bellied stove. Her mother had kept her cook stove busy too, with fruit pies in their flaky homemade crusts and ten layer molasses cakes spread with fresh apple butter. There would be banana pudding on Christmas Day with a homemade meringue topping and stockings filled with tangerines and chocolate crème drop candy.

The house had always been filled with friends and neighbors as well as children. Many children in the area didn't have such abundant treats at their own homes, and they would stop by for apples and the sweet taste of an exotic orange, a fruit many of them had never tasted before. And of course for the adults, there had been plenty of adult treats, for like Billy, her father, thought all holidays included drinking. At Christmas, there was usually a fresh run of moonshine to sell to pay for luxuries like crates of Florida oranges, and to use for hot toddies sprinkled with cinnamon and nutmeg. There would also be homemade eggnog, spiked for the adults, and lots of beer and good Kentucky bourbon for those who preferred it. But in spite of the drinking, the holidays were usually good times; her dad remained cheerful, and even though the presents had been few, the joy and sharing of love and good food had brought warmth and a lightness of spirit missing from the rest of the year.

Sighing, Tess stretched her arms overhead, her mind wondering. Christmas was still weeks away. She needed to slow down and take it one holiday at a time. For now, she needed to concentrate on Halloween. Sammy wanted to be a Ninja Turtle, his latest super hero craze. She chuckled when she tried to wrap her mind around the thought of a mutated teenage turtle super hero. It seemed kind of farfetched and she wondered whose mind had thought up of such a concept. But then she'd spent many childhood Saturday mornings watching Mighty Mouse and Underdog, and everyone knew neither a mouse nor a dog could fly or talk. So maybe it was true that the more things changed, the more they stayed the same.

Medical Record Department
Hospital Administration
Patient History:

This forty-three-year-old white male has a several year history of occasional indigestion treated with antacids. Patient states that about once a year, usually near the holidays, he goes on a big alcoholic binge and has severe epigastric pain. His general health has been otherwise good. He works daily and denies any food intolerance of any significance and no weight loss. On the night prior to this present admission, he was on a tremendous alcoholic binge and today while at work noted the sudden onset of severe epigastric pain, which became more generalized throughout the abdomen and particularly localized in the lower left quadrant, associated with a fairly ridged abdomen, nausea and vomiting with some blood tinged material and no relief of the symptoms. His co-workers brought him from the mines where he was taken by ambulance to see Dr. Sutherland who referred him to the hospital.

Physical Examination:

A well developed well nourished white male, acutely ill and dry.

Blood Pressure: 150/100; pulse 100; temperature 99

Heart: normal rhythm, no murmurs

Abdomen: ridged and tender in the epi-gastrium and left lower quadrant, no bowel sounds could be heard, no areas were palpable.

X-Ray: An upright film of the abdomen showed no evidence of free air.

Course:

Patient was taken from outpatient up to the operating room where he was promptly explored through an incision and found to have a perforated peptic ulcer. The perforation was closed and the patient was treated subsequently with lavine tube drainage and intravenous feedings. By the 3rd postoperative day the Levin tube was removed and patient began taking clear liquids by mouth. He promptly progressed to a soft diet and on the 7th postoperative day he was doing quite well and had no symptoms. The sutures were removed and the patient was discharged from the hospital.

# WHAT IS SECURITY?

When Tess pulled into the parking lot of the studio the next morning, she was surprised to see that Ross hadn't arrived yet. Taking out her keys, she unlocked the door and disarmed the alarm system. The building was cold so she adjusted the thermostat before tugging off her jacket. It seemed odd to be here without Ross on a Monday morning. She usually worked Saturday's alone or with Gina's help, but when Monday came, Ross was always in bright and early, eager to begin a new week.

Picking up the empty coffee pot, she headed to the back to rinse it and start a fresh pot of coffee, but as she passed Ross's desk, her eye caught the blinking of the red message indicator light on the phone. She paused and for some reason a chill ran down her spine and she shivered as she watched the silent blinking of the tiny light. She felt a foreboding that whatever message was there, she wouldn't want to hear it.

"Don't be silly," she scolded herself; it was probably just a customer inquiring about their work or needing to reschedule an appointment. Balancing the empty coffee pot in both hands, she juggled it up and down a few times contemplating ignoring the light; she could always tell Ross she hadn't noticed it. If it really was bad news, she didn't feel up to handling it until she'd had a cup of coffee. Then she panicked. *What if it was one of her kids and the school was trying to reach her?* The thought had her quickly banging the coffee pot down onto the desk and reaching for the phone. Just as her fingers touched it, she was startled by its shrill ring.

With sudden trembling hands, she dropped the receiver before getting it to her ear. Feeling foolish, she cleared her throat and brightly said, "Good morning, Posterity Studios, how may I help you?"

"Tess? Is that you? Did you get my message?"

Barely recognizing the soft voice, Tess replied teasingly, "I was just going to listen to it Becky. Are you calling to tell me that old man of yours is playing hooky this morning?" Becky was Ross's wife, a sweet, gentle, and soft spoken woman. Tess loved telling Ross that she was definitely his better half.

The other woman's voice broke on a sob as she replied, "We're at the hospital, Tess. He had a heart attack this morning, or at least they're pretty certain that's what it was."

Stunned by her words, Tess again had difficulty holding onto the phone, using both hands to keep it firmly pressed to her ear, she replied, "What? When? Why didn't you call me earlier?" She knew she wasn't being rational, but she still felt she must have heard wrong.

"I tried calling as soon as I could but you must've already left to take Sammy to school. I left a message on your cell phone and on the machine there."

Tess stared guiltily at the blinking light before reaching out to hit the erase button. Her cell phone was buried in her purse, the ringer set to vibrate. She still wasn't used to carrying it and only kept it nearby when on an outside job, in case the kids needed to reach her. Closing her eyes and taking a deep breath to calm herself, she asked Becky for details. Listening carefully, the older woman nervously told her how Ross had awakened early with chest pain; it had grown worse as the sun rose until he was pale and sweaty and complaining of nausea. That was when she had ignored his protests and called the rescue squad.

Becky's voice dropped to a whisper, "Tess, honey, he looks bad. I'm really scared."

Tess squeezed her eyes shut to prevent the sudden rush of hot tears from overflowing, her heart going out to the other woman. Becky was an orphan and she and Ross had no children; she had no one to turn to in a time of crisis. Tess and the other staff of the studio were the closest thing to family she had after Ross. Wanting to be there for her and for Ross, her first thought was to simply close up the shop and rush to the hospital. But she knew her boss too well. She knew his first worry would be his business and his financial situation. He was a hard-working man of fierce pride and he had always made it a priority to look out for Becky, to make sure she was taken care of. His next worry would be his credit status, always paying his bills on time or ahead of schedule; it would crush his pride to see things getting behind because he was sick.

The thoughts flashed through her mind swiftly as she quickly came to a decision. "Becky, just hang in there. I'll call Bobby and Gina and get them in here to mind the shop and I'll be there as soon as I can to sit with you, okay?" Bobby was an assistant who usually came in after lunch and worked through the busiest part of the day. He knew the business almost as well as she did, so she knew he and Gina could handle things. "Tell Ross that it will be business as usual here, so he doesn't need to worry about anything; not you, not the shop, not his finances. We have it all under control and I don't want him concentrating on anything but getting well." She swallowed past the lump in her throat. "And Becky, he's a tough old bird; he'll get through this. Just stay calm, okay?"

She pulled the daily schedule from the top drawer as she placed the cordless phone back on its charger. She noted that there wasn't anything out of the ordinary scheduled, nothing that Bobby and Gina together couldn't handle, at least until the evening appointments started arriving, but she planned to be back for those.

Monday, Wednesday, and Thursday evenings and Saturday mornings were reserved for appointments for sittings and portrait previews to give busy two paycheck families a chance to come in together without anyone having to take time off from work. There were two appointments for previews scheduled for early evening. She generally alternated the extra hours with Ross so that no one was stuck with too many long days in a row, but for now she would just have to cope on her own, or maybe she could get Bobby to cover some extra hours, with the holidays coming, he might like the extra income. At this time of year, it was best to keep everyone a satisfied customer so she didn't want to start juggling the schedule too much by postponing appointments. Nibbling at the tender flesh on the inside of her lower lip, she decided she would wait to see exactly how bad Ross's condition truly was before she made any major decisions about the schedule. They just needed to get through today and then she could assess the situation and plot a course of action.

She sighed heavily as she dropped into Ross's desk chair, closing her eyes for a moment to calm the overwhelmed feeling that threatened to reduce her to a mass of nerves. This was no time for a panic attack; no time for second guessing herself. She wasn't alone in this. Bobby and Gina were very dependable, and she'd been Ross's right arm for several years now; she knew the business inside and out.

First things first, she needed to sort out what was a priority and what could be put on a back-burner for a few days. Pulling out a pad, she jotted some notes. Calling Bobby and Gina was at the top of the list, and next would be making sure one of the older kids were home for Sammy after school. She couldn't remember if Chad was scheduled to work or not, but someone would also have to make dinner since she would have to be back at the shop no later than five thirty for the evening appointments.

And she would have to find Ross's notes for those appointments; Mondays and Thursdays were usually his late days, with Wednesday evening and Saturday mornings making up her extra hours. He would have notes on anything in particular mentioned during the actual sittings that the customer might be interested in. She would need those to make sure she didn't miss an added sale or stumble over her tongue while talking with the customers. Taking a moment to rest her face in her hands, she whispered a silent prayer for Ross's health and for guidance in running his business, "Lord, please don't let me screw this up!" With a sigh, she reached for the phone; item number one—call Bobby.

Much later after her long day at the hospital with Becky, and then her evening back at the studio, Tess was almost too tired to drive home. Chad had taken the night off and his boss had been so sympathetic to the situation that he'd given them free pizza for dinner, so she was greeted to the sweet aroma of yeast dough and tomato sauce when she walked in the door.

"I just popped two slices in the microwave when I saw you pull in," Tressa told her as she hung her jacket and coat on the rack. Tess smiled in amazement as she looked around the kitchen; surprised to find it neat and somewhat clean, instead of the usual mess they left it in when left alone in the evenings. "Chad's helping Sammy with his bath, and I just put the teakettle on so you can make a cup of tea or hot chocolate if you want." Tressa was talking very rapidly as she nervously moved around the kitchen.

"Hot chocolate would be great. Maybe one of the gourmet flavors I've been saving. I'm so tired, I need a treat tonight!" She watched as her daughter went to the pantry to retrieve the cocoa mix feeling somewhat overwhelmed and amazed at her uncomplaining cooperation and her kindness. Ross often accused her of being too protective, of not allowing them to rely more on themselves. Maybe he was right, maybe they could handle more responsibility than she gave them credit for, but the most important thing was that they were coming through for her now. "Oh, and Tressa," she paused, waiting for her daughter to turn a questioning gaze to her before she smiled and said, "Thank you!" They shared a rare moment of bonding before a wet bundle of boy suddenly wrapped himself around her legs, a wet trail leading back through the kitchen to the hallway.

"Sorry, Mom, the little monkey escaped!" Chad apologized as he trotted after his brother, towel in hand. His shirt and jeans were wet from his brother's splashing and she smiled her thanks up to him before unwrapping a slippery wet Sammy from her legs.

"You're home, you're home!" Sam chanted, bouncing against her legs, "I missed you!" She pulled him up to receive his hug and his wet smacking kiss. "Chad made me take a bath. I didn't want to. I wanted to wait for you but he made me." He cast an accusing stare at his brother but before he could continue his fussing, she diverted him by asking about his homework. "It's all done. Chad made me do it." Clearly, he felt his older brother had betrayed him tonight. "Oh, come see my project. Come on, you gotta see!" Sammy tugged at her hands, "Chad and TT helped me." He had called his sister Tree Tree when he'd first started talking, which over the years had been shortened to TT and now it was his private name for her.

Giving into his eagerness, she followed him back to his bedroom where her eyes widened and she didn't know whether to giggle or cry at what he proudly displayed. Using Popsicle sticks and a shoebox, they had made a rough log cabin with cutouts of people glued to the sides. "It's great isn't it? It's for history class." It was rough and certainly not done with the patience she would have crafted it, but it was after all a child's school project, and should have been constructed to his idea of perfection, not her own.

Looking embarrassed, Chad explained that the teacher's note had instructed to either write a report or do a project, and while Sammy had wanted them to help him write a report, the log cabin seemed easier. She nearly smiled; Chad would not have had the patience to wait for his brother to write a report, not as slow as Sammy wrote.

Her older son shrugged. "He was a little upset with us at first, but when he saw how it turned out, he decided he liked it. I came up with the idea 'cause I remembered you and Uncle Grant helped me make one as a project one year. Yours was better than this, but hopefully this will do in a pinch." He was blushing and stammering; they seldom helped Sammy with his schoolwork and usually complained when she asked. Pride swelled in her chest as she realized they had come through for her and had leaned on each other when she hadn't been able to be there with them.

"I think it'll do just fine, don't you, Sam?" She tousled his hair as he snuggled against her legs. Then she reached out over his head to hug her oldest. Planting a soft peck on his cheek, she whispered, "Thank you, you really came through for me."

Sam was nodding his agreement, holding his arms out for her to pick him up which she could barely do any more, and she shook her head as she balanced him on her hip, his legs dangling near her knees. "You ready for bed?" she asked.

Tess had him say good night to his siblings before she wrestled him into his pajamas and tucked him into the lower bunk. She kissed his cheeks and brought him a glass of water before finally turning out the light, the enticing smell of hot pizza drawing her back to the kitchen.

Chad and Tressa joined her at the table as she ate, quietly relating the details of their evening. When she pushed her plate away, she told them what she and Becky had been told at the hospital. "It was a heart attack; they're not certain how much damage has been done yet, but he'll be having tests to look for possible causes. He's probably looking at several weeks' recovery."

She watched their faces as she talked, noting not only the concern but there was something more—something that seemed to indicate fear. And while they liked Ross, he was like another uncle to them, she sensed it was more than that; maybe it was just that they realized his death could destroy any sense of financial security they had. "I asked Gina to place an AD to hire extra help. We usually hire holiday help around this time each year anyway, but even if I find someone right away, it's still going to mean a lot of extra hours for me, so I will have to count on you two to help me out around here."

They both assured her that they were there for her. Glancing at his sister, Chad cleared his throat before he said, "You know, Mom, I've been thinking"—he nervously twirled a toothpick between his fingers while he talked—"on the days that I have to work, why don't I pick Sam and Tressa up after school and bring them to the studio. They could do their homework and Tressa could possibly help out at the shop if you need her."

His sister nodded her agreement. "That way, you won't miss those extra hours we always have together in the evenings and you can still check Sam's homework and all. Sam could watch cartoons on the little TV in Ross's office if he got bored and I could answer the phone and act as the receptionist for you."

Tess carefully studied their faces. They had really thought this through and they were right. She usually came home for a few hours at the end of the school day, going back to the shop after dinner when she had evening hours, but now she would have to stay until the closing of regular business hours and still manage to have the evening appointments covered. She felt tired just thinking about it. She sighed, "You're right, you're both right. I hadn't thought that far ahead yet. This is really gonna take some juggling to make sure everything is covered. I'll have to talk to Bobby and Gina and see if they are willing to take on more hours."

They sat in silence for a few minutes as Tess turned possibilities over in her head. "Well, it will all work I guess. For now guys, thank you for your help! And now, I'm going to get ready for bed."

Chad buzzed her cheek as he rose from his chair. "Just let us know what you need Mom, we'll help as much as we can."

Tressa rose too. "I've got homework, but Chad's right, just let us know."

She rose and hugged them both goodnight. "I love you guys so much, and I'm proud of you." As she carried her dishes to the sink, she shook her head in amazement; she couldn't ever remember getting their unsolicited, uncomplaining support before, at least not since they'd become teenagers. As she rinsed her cup before stacking it in the dishwasher, it hit her—the thing that was really at the core of their sudden desire to help her. It went deeper than concern for Ross, how naïve of her to think that was it. The reality was they had both suddenly seen how fragile the security of their lives was; she represented their security and if Ross could have a heart attack, then so could she. True, Ross was fifteen years her senior, but to a teenager, they were of the same generation—old. She would have to reassure them that she was in good health, but that should anything ever happen to her, she had made plans for their continued support, both financially and emotionally; Grant and Patty were prepared to give them a home if the need ever arose, with no children of their own they treated them almost as grandchildren. And after the divorce when she had realized that she was all they had to depend on, she had purchased a large life insurance policy on herself and the monthly premium was one payment she never thought of skipping, no matter how tight the budget was.

The fragility of the thin veneer of security that people kept woven around them was that of an eggshell anyway. In a world so filled with calamity, disaster could strike in an instant. However, she longed to keep the reality of how quickly it could all be swept away from them for a little while longer.

# BELIEVE

October 26

As children, we love the adults in our lives for the care they give and the security they provide. As we become adults, the elder generation still represents a form of security for as long as there is an older generation, we have a sense of permanency. They give us someone to go to for advice and guidance even when we fail to follow that advice, and they give us someone to assure us that there is a purpose in living, a reason for our births, as well as someone to blame for the ails of the world.

I have been thinking about the generations of people that came before me. Sometimes they seem so far removed from me and my life and yet genetically and biologically, they are so very close. To say "my grandma's grandma" seems so long ago, so far removed, and I would imagine that I am something she never envisioned. And yet, my own grandchild will be able to say that about my grandma and that doesn't seem far away or long removed at all. In fact, my grandma passed away just ten years ago, so it will only be a matter of twenty to thirty years before that fifth generation comes along. A century truly is a short span of time and a lifetime merely a breath of air in the midst of a windstorm.

If I try to look ahead at future generations that will result from my own children, I find it mind boggling. We are so caught up in the here and now that we forget that it is only for a moment that we are allowed to make our mark upon the world; only for a moment and then it is gone. The only permanent marks are the genes we pass on to tomorrow's children. Children that will live in a world even more advanced than our own, children who will see and do things we only dream of, just as we do things our ancestors would have called magic, witchcraft, or worse.

There is no security, no answer to the meaning of life. All one can do is live it well and never take it for granted. Security must come from inside or all is madness. To think and truly realize that we float in space on a big blue marble amidst millions and millions of other masses not so unlike our own; totally dependent on our exact orbit around the sun to sustain life as we know it, with nothing to hold us there or secure us into place except an invisible force called gravity. Well, you realize that to believe is the only security we have.

But to believe in what? In a divine being who in his mercy allows us to stay "secure" in our orbit; to believe in someone or something larger and more powerful than we are that has the answers, that knows why we live and breathe and why we die. The alternative is madness.

I sometimes think of the astronauts who went to the moon. I imagine myself there, standing on the moon, looking out into all that vast, vast blackness surrounding me and seeing the earth—my home, my world—just floating out there amidst the blackness; just a speck against all the endless expanse of space around it, like a bubble floating in a glass of cola, suspended in the darkness, and I know that to have seen this and to truly witness how fragile our world is would have driven me over the brink into insanity. Especially, so knowing, that my only way back home—back to the security of my home—was a man-made ship that would have suddenly seemed so fragile and flimsy when placed against the eternity of space. I think I would have died then and there of fear.

Perhaps it was the same when Columbus sailed towards the "ends of the earth" in his ship, out into the unknown, and even though he sailed into the vastness of the ocean—which is very minute when compared with the vastness of space—it would have amounted to the same; sailing off into the vast unknown, the uncharted. Are they fools or heroes? Perhaps they already knew what it has taken me so long to discover: there is no security except for that which comes from within.

Following her nightly ritual, Tess looked in on the kids before heading for bed. Tressa lay curled around a large stuffed cat, one small hand tucked beneath her chin; her mass of dark curls nearly covering her face. Brushing the curls back from her daughter's face, she planted her nightly kiss. Tressa was petite like her grandmother and she'd inherited her grandmother's fiery temper as well. Combined with the streak of independence that she'd gotten from Tess, it made her a handful. Standing just over five feet tall, she herself was small boned, but Tressa hadn't yet reached the five feet mark and her bone structure could only be described as delicate. With small feet and tiny hands with long delicate fingers, it was hard to think of her as almost "grown up." People were often fooled by her appearance into believing she was meek and mild mannered, but if they crossed her it didn't take them long to realize how wrong they were. Tess knew her petite stature would bring out the protective instinct in most guys and she pitied the man who would ever think he could "tame" her. Tressa would always be her own individual.

Both boys were large boned like Billy, and it wouldn't be long before Sammy towered over her as Chad already did. Tressa had inherited her curls from Billy while the boys had Tess's straight hair. All three had inherited the dimple in her chin, a mark that came from her maternal grandpa. It seemed odd to not only have the genes of a man she'd never met, but also to have passed those genes on to her own children.

After tucking the covers more securely around Sammy, she moved on to her own room, sighing as she pulled her old flannel nightgown over her head, she felt very lonely tonight. Ross's brush with death made her think of all that was missing in her own life as well as all she had to be thankful for, like her children. Her life was hard, but good. She had three wonderful children, and in spite of her fights with Tressa and her concerns over Chad, she knew that they were good people and that warmed her heart.

Still there were nights when she cried alone in her bed. The kids were growing up fast and they weren't as close as they once had been. After her divorce from Billy and they were on their own for the first time, just the four of them, she'd called them the four musketeers. They had done everything together and she had never given much thought to the future when they would begin to exclude her in order to join their friends. She knew it was a natural process, a part of their growth; they had to grow away from her in order to become independent, but still it left her feeling empty inside. And while she knew it wasn't fair to expect them to fill the voids in her own life, she still missed them and all that they had once shared. If there was a special someone in her life to share it all with then perhaps it would be easier. But just as they had to become independent and grow away from her in order to carve their own niches in the fabric of life, she had to find a way to fill the voids on her own.

If being hated and rebelled against for her rules and restrictions was part of the job of parenting, then so be it. Her one consolation was that, some day, they would be mature enough to realize that it all came from her love for them and not some perverted desire to "ruin all their fun" as Tressa had told her more than once.

"Just because you have such a boring life, it doesn't mean you have to spoil all my fun!" She had yelled at Tess just a few weeks before when she refused to budge on her 10:00 p.m. curfew. "All you care about is your stupid job. I hope I never get as old and boring as you!"

The words had wounded Tess deeply since without the "stupid" job, they wouldn't survive, but she had merely sighed and calmly replied, "I hope you do. I would hate to think of the alternative to growing old. There's only one option you know."

The response had surprised Tressa and left her speechless and the fight had ended. She had known her mom was referencing her Uncle Wesley, who had taken his own life before his twenty-fifth birthday. So this round in their mother-daughter battle had ended as suddenly as it had begun.

Tess tried to be understanding. She remembered fights with her own mother and the feelings of being all alone and misunderstood that she knew Tressa must feel. Hell, she still felt that way most of the time, but she no longer blamed her mother.

After washing and moisturizing her face, she crawled into bed, but as she lay there staring into the darkness, the room seemed to fill with menacing shadows. Her loneliness made her feel small and vulnerable. Scolding herself she tried to settle down to sleep, but the feeling of uneasiness wouldn't pass. Instead of relaxing, her body seemed to fill with tension, and she realized she was gripping the covers tightly with both hands. With a sigh combined of frustration at her own nonsense and relief at finally giving in, she threw back the covers and ran down the hallway to the bathroom. Clicking the switch by the door, she felt relief when light poured over her, relieving the dark shadows of the hallway and flowing to the edges of her bedroom as well. Leaving her door open when she padded back to bed, she relaxed as the soft glow reached into the darkness and pushed the shadows back. Curling around her pillow, looking small and vulnerable and very like Tressa, she finally slept.

# Soldiers

The days passed swiftly in a blur of work for Tess. She was able to hire an assistant with studio experience and discovered that Gina knew much more about the photography work than she had realized so she was able to turn most of the portrait work over to the two of them. Bobby had agreed to work extra hours, including evening hours, to assist her with the sittings and viewings, and even volunteered to do some of the outside jobs on weekends, even though he normally didn't work weekend hours. Tess felt the tension slowly leave her body as things seemed to be falling into a manageable pattern.

Ross's heart attack hadn't been that severe, but multiple blockages had been found around his heart, including a defective valve. The doctors were able to repair the blockages via catheter but he'd undergone open heart surgery for the valve replacement. He had recovered quickly and had surprisingly gone home only a few days after the surgery. When Tess visited him, he seemed to be in good spirits; although thin and seeming to have aged ten years since the surgery. He told anyone who would listen how thankful he was to be alive. It made her feel good to know that Posterity's continued smooth operation had kept money worries from his mind, and she was glad she'd been able to do that for him.

She'd been struggling to put together the video footage for Ms. Kirkenbaum but she hadn't confessed her frustrations to Ross. She wanted to prove to him that she could handle it all on her own. While she knew the basics about the equipment, she had never really used it, so she found she lost most of the arguments when she attempted to fight with it. The other recent video shoots had been straight forward productions that only required simple edits—bloopers removed, titles and music added—but Ms. Kirkenbaum's footage required more. She was being very understanding, but Tess knew she needed a final product in time to use for her last minute holiday ads. She wanted the results to be at Ross's usual high quality, but since it was a first effort for her, she wanted it to be special—something that flowed with color and sound, something fun to watch, pleasing to the eye, and that showcased her own creative ability.

With a sigh she pushed those thoughts from her mind; she didn't want to think about that frustration tonight. She smiled thinking of the recent strength and dependability she'd discovered in her two oldest offspring and what a pleasant surprise it was. They helped her with the cooking and cleaning and looked after Sammy without being asked. On the days Chad worked, he brought his siblings to the studio where Tressa had proven to be of tremendous help, answering the phone and ringing up walk-in customers. She had a pleasing telephone voice and had surprised everyone with her ability to stay calm even when all four lines rang at once. Amazingly, she had even used her tremendous computer skills to create an updated customer database that made file retrieval so much faster and easier. Tess made sure to pay her a small compensation since her help had been much needed and appreciated as the busy season started. With Thanksgiving right around the corner, people were starting to schedule their holiday portraits.

Putting away the last of the dinner dishes, Tess stretched her back and hung the dish towel over the rack. It was good fortune that she'd been able to hire Mandy, the new shop assistant, to have time to get her somewhat familiar with things before the rush started. As it stood now, the poor girl had had to learn most things on the run, and it would just keep getting worse until Christmas was over. Mandy had been a trooper and within a couple of days, it seemed as if she'd been there forever. Tess had christened her a Christmas angel, sent a couple of months early. But Gina had dubbed her their Halloween haunt since the girl had painted bright orange stripes in her hair to celebrate the season.

Now it was Friday evening, and for the first time in weeks, she was alone. There'd been no time for long hot baths or soothing cups of hot chocolate, no quiet moments to write in her journal or reflect on the past, but tonight was her night. Chad and Tressa had gone to the football game and Grant and Patty had taken Sammy for pizza and a movie. The house was hers with at least two hours of blissful peace and quiet. She hadn't even turned the television on; she wanted nothing to disrupt the quiet. First, she was going to take a bubble bath—with bubbles so thick they would coat the tub for ages even after the water was drained. Then she was going to mix a cup of hot chocolate and settle down with her journal as she felt like writing tonight. Her head was full of memories.

November 5

Becca called tonight just after Grant and Patty left with Sam. Grant had called her earlier and told her about Ross's heart attack, so she called to see how I was coping. It seems we never get to spend much time together, we both lead such busy lives and yet, she's my best friend. We share a common past, as if we are both survivors of a war. She saw more battles than I did, but we both carry the scars.

We discussed all the ways Daddy used to make us feel inferior to other people's children; we were always less important and always had to give into cousins and other visitors. They were always right in any childish conflict, always better behaved in his eyes; we were always in the wrong, always less somehow. Of course, we were less when compared to him as well. I remember trips to the grocery store where he would treat himself to a Nehi Redpop and a Milky Way bar and enjoy them in front of us while we were seldom allowed "store bought" treats like chocolate and soda pop. The message was that we weren't worth the expense. Mom was treated the same way. I never remember seeing him buy her a soda, or for that matter, allowing her any simple purchase a woman might enjoy such as sweet smelling bath powder or face cream. She even had to show him her worn bras and undergarments before he would give her money to purchase new ones.

Of course, at other times, he could be very generous. I remember occasionally sharing 3 Musketeers bars and sipping from the small, green glass bottles of Coca Cola with him. When I was around four, after his ulcer operation, he had to make daily trips to the hospital to have the drainage tubes cleaned and he would take me along with him. Afterwards, we would stop at the drugstore where they sold candy by the pound and he would buy a half pound of chocolate covered peanuts for us to share. He would tease with the clerk and tell her that some day he and I were going to Japan to eat chocolate covered ants. I always felt proud to be included in his plans, even though I was certain I didn't want to eat ants, covered in chocolate or not. As I have said, there were many facets to the man I called Daddy, and he seemed to mellow somewhat in the last few years before his death and even expressed regrets to my mother for the harshness he had shown us.

Shortly after my birth, my mom had fallen into a depression that lasted several years. I guess coping with the farm work, the older children and an abusive, alcoholic husband was all she could handle. She didn't need a newborn added to the mix, especially since Wesley was eight when I was born. It had to be stressful to think of starting over with a baby. The doctor's called it a nervous breakdown and she was hospitalized twice during the first three years of my life, though I am sure it was postpartum blues as we now know this sadness to be.

Then they just labeled her "off in the head." After these episodes, Daddy always treated her as if she were slow mentally, especially when it came to money or business transactions such as buying a car or even purchasing new furniture. He never allowed her a say in any of that.

Because of Mom's illness, much of my early care was left to Becca, so she and I became very close. She tolerated my terrible twos and answered all of my "whys." She bathed me, fed me, and even swatted my rear a few times. As we grew older, she became more of a mentor and I longed to be just like her, an intelligent, pretty young lady. Although my dad's relatives would tease me and tell me I would never measure up.

When I was around ten, I remember she told me that as I grew older, the gap in our ages would shrink. At the time, I had no idea what she meant, but of course, she was right. As I became an adult, the years between us seemed to melt away so that I no longer view her as a parental figure. To me, she's now just Becca—my sister.

We talked about Wesley tonight too, which is something we never do. Even after all these years, the memories still hurt as the three of us were close. On Sunday mornings, we would walk to church and Sunday school together which was a two-mile walk each way. Coming home, the trip was almost all uphill, but they would turn it into a game for me so that before I knew it, we were home. Sometimes we would each carefully count our footsteps and measure how far each of us could walk in exactly one hundred steps. Or they would quiz me on nursery rhymes or my multiplication tables, although at the time, I didn't realize it was multiplication. They would just tell me to recite my "twos" or my "fives" and I would chant what I had been taught. It was just a game to me, like the nursery rhymes I had memorized, only with numbers.

Near town, the road was hard topped, cut from the hillside, hanging a precarious thirty feet above the river. Traffic and pedestrians were protected from the steep bank by a long chain link fence, concreted right into the sidewalk that ran its length. The remaining rock face on the opposite side of the road still showed the drill marks where the engineers had drilled holes into the steep cliff side in order to drop in dynamite to blast away enough of the rock to build the road bank. The cliff side was always wet with underground water seeping between the rock formations. As we would walk through this area, I liked to drag a stick against the fence and listen to the sound bounce against the cliff wall; the wetness softened the echo so that it sounded like a forest waterfall.

When we reached the turn onto our road, which was an unpaved gravel road, if the weather was warm, I would remove my patent leather shoes and white anklets to walk barefoot. The dirt on the well worn road was hard packed, and in some areas, worn as smooth as a piece of glass so that it felt cool against my feet. Wesley would tease me and tell me I had feet as tough as leather, but Becca would assure me that he was only teasing and if Becca said it, I knew that it was true.

I loved our Sunday walks. I always felt so loved walking along between the two of them. Becca was my mentor and Wesley was my hero when he wasn't picking on me! They never showed any sibling rivalry towards me, and if there was any true jealousy from them, I never felt it. Instead, they made me feel as if my birth had been a special gift from God. So in spite of my alcoholic father, I grew up feeling I was special in some way.

Our Sunday dinners were huge affairs with many of the neighborhood children stopping by. Everyone loved my momma's fried chicken and mashed potatoes or her steaming pots of chicken and dumplings. Being farmer's children we always had plenty to eat, but many children in the area weren't so fortunate so they always showed up for Sunday dinner where they knew they could get a belly full of hot, delicious food. Of course, no one ever stayed to help clean up. According to Daddy, they were guests, even if they were uninvited, so Becca would have to clean up alone while the others chose up sides for games of Red Rover or hide-and-seek. I usually stayed in the kitchen and helped by rinsing the dishes for her and Wesley would sometimes dry for us. Grant never helped out in the kitchen; that was "women's work," although I don't think Patty would let him get by with that excuse now. He was usually away from the house until dusk on Sundays anyway. Sometimes, he visited with Grandma, but more often, he was with his older friends romping through the woods playing games of Fox and Hound or hunting for dry land fish.

Becca would frequently recite poetry as she washed up or recite lines to us from the latest play her drama class was performing at school. She loved drama and literature and it still seems she remembers everything she has ever read. She can recite more authors than I can even name. Other times Wesley would strum his guitar and Becca would sing along with him; like Momma, she had a lovely singing voice and the ability to sweetly carry a tune, an accomplishment I've never been able to achieve. Of course, at that age, I hadn't yet discovered my ineptitude and I would yell out the words along with her sweet, soft singing. She was the anchor in my life, and when Momma was stressed out and Daddy was drunk, she somehow made the fear less. I realize now what a child she was and how scared and alone she must have felt herself. I'm glad she had Wesley. Even though he was younger, he was someone to turn to; he was another soldier there enduring the battle with her.

Being the next oldest, Wesley actually played with me. Of course, he also teased me and did all those things big brothers are supposed to do to torture their little sisters. I often followed him around as he did his chores, more nuisance than help I'm sure, but I longed for his approval and just to be near him.

At the top of the hillside above our house were the hayfields where the alfalfa and sweet clover grew. Thinking of them, I remember one Sunday afternoon when Wes had been sent to gather the fresh cut hay before the rain came and ruined it as it lay in the fields. I tagged along and stayed behind as he went to haul the first load to the barn. I remember standing there all alone amidst the grasses, my long hair whipping about my face as the wind rolled over the mountain tops. The only sounds were the whispers of the wind in my hair and the gentle rustle of the leaves as it blew through the treetops. Around me I could hear the steady hum of the bees droning as they worked the sweet clover, busy pollinating the fields and my father's crops.

Staring out at the blue crests of the mountains in the distance, I felt as if I were the only person on earth and if I stood really, really still, it seemed as if I could feel the earth moving beneath my feet. Holding my arms out to shoulder height, I started turning in circles, faster and faster, until I fell into the fragrant grass. As I lay there looking up at the pristine blue sky overhead, I was certain that I could now feel the movement of the whole world turning forward, just for me, carrying me off into the future. Squeezing my eyes shut I watched the patterns that danced against my eyelids. I thought about my Sunday school class earlier that day and the cute little boy I sat next to each week.

"God," I softly whispered, "are you listening? Well, if you are, I just wanted to ask you to take care of me all my life. Help me be good and find good; I don't want to be bad or do bad things and have to live with the devil. So God, show me what I should do to be good and I'll try to do it. Ms. Veronica at Sunday school said we didn't have to be perfect, we just had to believe, and God I do believe in you."

Opening my eyes, I blinked at the sudden brightness and

then tightly closed them back to add the true purpose of my prayer, "Oh, and God, one more thing, Howie Bradley is so cute, can you let him be my boyfriend? In Jesus name I pray, Amen!" Satisfied with my prayer, I plucked a straw of sweet grass to chew on. Absentmindedly chattering to myself, I envisioned a future where Howie and I were married. We would build our house right there on the exact same spot where I lay, at the top of the world, so nothing bad could reach us or touch us, and any time we wanted to, we could lie back in the grass and look up at the face of God where he would always be close, protecting us.

"Buzz, buzz, buzz, Tess and Howie sitting in a tree, k-i-s-s-i-n-g." Wesley's dark shadow loomed over me, and too late I noticed the jingle of the mules harness signaling his return. He made a kissing sound with his mouth and I jumped to my feet and kicked out at him.

"Stop it, stop teasing me right now!"

Wes laughed as I lashed out at him, and soon our arguing turned into a game of chase where he finally allowed me to tackle him and tickle him in the soft grass. When he finally swore to take it all back, I let him up and we returned to our work.

Finishing with that field, we move to the next where some of the cut grass had been raked into haystacks, the rest lying as it had fallen. With his pitchfork, Wes raked the straw and loaded it into the box-type wagon the mule was harnessed to. Being equipped with sled runners instead of wheels, it easily navigated the rough mountain terrain and could glide smoothly over the gravel roads and rocky hillsides. My job was to climb up into the wagon box and tramp down the sweet grass as Wesley tossed it in. I was probably just a nuisance being too small to make much difference, but Wes was always patient with me, and convinced me that I did a good job.

Wes had allowed me to take the reins even though I could barely see out of the sled box to the mules' head. With a straw of grass hanging from his mouth and his shirtless torso glimmering with sweat, he lounged beside me and asked while tickling my nose with a straw, "Tess, who do you love most in the whole wide world?"

I giggled, brushing away the straw. This was a game we played often, so I knew the answer he expected, "You!" I yelled as loudly as I could. Wesley liked being loved the most by everyone and he seemed to need a lot of reassurance.

"Who?" he asked again, cupping a hand by his ear, as if he hadn't heard me.

"You!" I yelled again, bouncing in the straw to give emphasis to my answer.

"Spell it."

"Y-O-U! With a capital Y!" I yelled out the answer, just the way I knew he liked for me to.

He ruffled my hair and took the reins back from my small hands to navigate the tight turn into our barnyard. "I love you too, squirt."

*As I said, Wesley was my hero. Thinking about him still hurts and yet it was good to talk about him with Becca tonight. I thought I would go insane at first when he died. It was my first loss as a young adult; my first loss of someone so close to my own age. But more than that, it was the loss of my childhood playmate, my big brother—my hero. And the saddest part of it all was that he chose to leave; he chose to leave all of us, even though I know he loved us. He loved us all dearly. He cried over our pain like it was his own, but for Wesley, the pain of staying was too great.*

*There are times when I can barely remember his face, and at other times, it seems like it was only yesterday and I can almost hear him asking, "Who do you love?"*

November 6

Success! I went in early this morning and finally finished the video for Ms. Kirkenbaum. I had been having issues with the mixer, but I finally discovered what I'd been doing wrong and then everything just came together. Mandy delivered it after work today, so now I'll have butterflies in my tummy all weekend waiting to hear if she liked it.

*Talking with Becca last night left my head full of the past and this morning, I awoke with a memory of one winter morning that was so crisp and fresh in my mind that I almost expected to pull back the curtains and see snow.*

*It was a memory from before I was school age, maybe four or five. We awoke one morning to a fresh snowfall that had fallen quietly over night, a heavy wet snow that loaded the branches and pulled them earthward creating hidden caves of white beneath, guarded by monstrous statues that were created by the patterns of the snow as it lay in the branches. The sun had risen on a world so pristine bright that it hurt the eyes to look upon it and the rugged mountain roads were definitely impassable for school buses, so Wes and Becca were home for the day.*

*Before leaving for work, Daddy told Momma that after breakfast to have Wesley turn the mule and the milk cow out of their stalls and shovel them out since he was home for the day. The fresh snow was more temptation than I could bear, so bundling up like a little Eskimo, I tagged along behind him. The sun's glare on the brightness of the snow was blinding at first but the air had the crisp, clean, fresh feeling that comes after a storm, and it made me feel like running and dancing with joy. It was little wonder to me that old Hank, our mule, seemed to feel the same way. He snorted and tossed his head impatiently as Wes and I entered the barn. In winter, he had to stay inside most of the time and it made him irritable and frisky.*

*As we passed his stall to let Bessie—our milk cow—out, Hank reached out to nip at Wesley's jacket, snorting in protest that the cow was getting attention first. "In a minute," Wes told him, smacking him on the nose, "you'll get your turn."*

*I watched as Bessie plodded from her stall and went to stand calmly by the fence. The wind had drifted the snow against a fence post and the weight of the snow had trapped a cluster of weeds and grasses that grew along the roadway and pushed them through the fence where the cow could reach them with her big soft lips. She munched contently, her fat brown tail softly swishing happily from side to side.*

*Wes tossed Hank some ears of corn before taking a shovel into the dark interior of Bessie's stall to begin the odorous task of shoveling out her waste. I soon grew impatient for him to be finished; I wanted him to come and play in the snow with me. Bored, I scrambled up the ladder to the hayloft and jumped down over and over again, repeatedly asking, "How much longer? Are you almost done?"*

*He just laughed and answered from inside the stall, "Soon, baby, I promise."*

*"But the snow's gonna melt and then it'll be all muddy and we won't be able to play!" I complained. Hank let out a long donkey-like bray, adding his protest to mine. "See? Hank wants to play too!"*

*Sighing, Wes scooped me up and sat me near the top of the ladder to the hayloft. "Stay there while I let him out. I'll shovel his stall at the same time and we'll only have to empty the wheelbarrow once." The droppings were shoveled and loaded into the wheelbarrow and then wheeled to a compost pile at the far end of the pasture. Wesley usually made two trips, putting Bessie back into her stall before he turned Hank out. That was the way Daddy had taught him and we were to soon find out why.*

*I clung to the top rung of the ladder, watching as he swung the door to Hank's stall open, quickly jumping behind it to be out of reach as the frisky mule lunged from his stall, bucking and snorting his way out into the sunshine. I laughed as he alternately threw his body into the air and then kicked his strong legs out behind him. Then suddenly before I realized his intentions, he ran right over to Bessie and using his thick neck, strong from wearing a collar to pull the plow and the hay wagon in summer, he shoved her face down into the snow. Stunned by his actions I froze for a moment, waiting for him to let her go, but several seconds passed and he just stood there, holding her face down in the snow.*

*Jumping from the ladder, I ran screaming for Wesley who rushed from the dark interior of the stall and paused as his eyes adjusted to the brightness of the sunshine, streaming in from the open eaves at the front of the barn. I remember the shocked expression on his face as he realized what Hank was doing and he shouted as he ran to try and save the cow.*

*The ornery old mule first kicked out at Wes, who yelled for me to stay back away from his strong hind legs. Managing to dodge the flying hooves, he tried to grab the mule's neck, but sensing Wesley's intentions Hank turned to nip at him with his teeth, which meant he had to momentarily release his hold on Bessie, which gave her a chance to draw in a breath of air before he again shoved her face back into the snow.*

*Wes was only about twelve years old at the time and his small arms were no match for Hank's strength, but his continued tugging must have annoyed the cantankerous mule because, suddenly, he turned and butted Wesley in the chest with his hard as a rock head. As Wesley went sprawling in the snow, Bessie again had a chance to take in some oxygen.*

*"Run you dumb old cow!" I shouted, "Run!" But she just stood there, gasping air until once again her face was shoved back into the snow. Not knowing what else to do since Wes and Bessie seemed to be losing the battle, I ran screaming for Momma.*

*I don't remember where Uncle Grant was that day, but at my shouts Momma and Becca came running. Momma had her broom in her hands and together we all yelled and screamed as she whacked Hank's backside until suddenly, as if annoyed by a swarm of pesky flies, Hank snorted in disgust and released the cow before calmly walking back to his stall. After all the excitement, Bessie drew in several deep breaths and then turned to finish munching the dried grass, leaving the rest of us stunned at the calmness with which the animals had reacted to all the fuss.*

*On bright, snowy winter days, I think of old Hank. I don't believe he really intended to hurt Bessie on that long ago morning. I think he was just so filled with the joy of living, of drawing fresh clean air into his lungs that he had to shout it out the only way he could. Then there stood that dumb old cow quietly munching on a bunch of weeds. It probably seemed as if she wasn't appreciating things enough, at least not to Hank. I think he wanted to shake her up, scare her a little so she would appreciate being alive.*

*I feel that way myself at times, so filled with the power of living that I want to sing and dance and give joy to our maker all at once. It's as if I can hold my hands out and grasp the very essence of life as it moves all around me, warming me, embracing me in its power. I too have longed to shake others who refuse to feel the warmth, the goodness of living, the love that surrounds us if we only look for it. There is so much joy in just living, in merely drawing breath into our lungs. It's impossible to explain, but old Hank would have understood.*

*I think maybe that's what everyone loved about Wesley, he cherished life. He loved everybody and wanted them to find the same joy in living that he did. He couldn't bear to see anyone hurt or depressed or lonely; he picked up stray human beings the way Patty picks up stray dogs. Everyone wanted to be close to Wes because he wouldn't allow you to just plod along down life's path watching your feet. He made you look up, see the sunshine and rejoice in the living.*

*The problem was that Wes couldn't seem to take his own advice and he could feel all of humanities' pain. At a party or a bar, Wes was the center of attention; he loved being around people. This is probably because when he was alone, the memories of his childhood were more than he could bear. Many nights he would drink until he passed out,* reading his Bible and questioning why God allowed bad things to happen to good people; he found it all very confusing.

I didn't find out until after his death that he had been sexually abused by our trusted childhood pediatrician for many years. The doctor was an icon in our area, praised for his philanthropy; especially after he founded an orphanage not too far from his office. Then, as now, this was a very impoverished area and he allowed parents who were down on their luck to leave their children for a few weeks or months if need be, until they were on their feet again. The orphanage provided food and shelter and he provided free medical care. Years later, I learned that he had abused many of the boys that had stayed at the orphanage, but no one would have believed an indigent, poor child in those days. They would have accused them of nefarious behavior or slander against a good man, so he was allowed to get away with the abuse for many, many years.

He also had an overnight clinic near his home, and since travel around the rough mountain roads was so tedious and difficult in those days, he would frequently find excuses for my parents to leave Wesley there. Looking back, you would think my parents would find it odd that Wesley needed to stay overnight for a high fever, but I did not. But at the time, they appreciated his diligence and care for their child.

The doctor had groomed Wesley slowly over many months, always being kind and understanding of the abuses of my father, but of course never reporting it or offering any real assistance. If he had, he might have lost access to Wesley. He gave Wes money and let him walk to the five-and-dime store to buy candy when he was supposed to be too sick to go home. He also bought him clothes and toys that Wes would never have gotten otherwise. I can even remember the good doctor visiting us late on a snowy Christmas Eve, spending hours traveling the treacherous roads just to bring a gift to his little buddy. He gave Wes the leather cowboy boots he had longed for; Wes loved the idea of being a cowboy, as did all little boys back then. Of course he brought gifts for me and Becca too, so as not to draw suspicion, but ours certainly were nothing as lavish as Wesley's boots. My parents excused it because Wes had broken two ribs early that fall and spent a week in the doctor's overnight clinic. They trusted anyone who seemed to be in authority, so they trusted the doctor explicitly. Turns out, they were wrong. But Wes carried the secret for many years and never confided in anyone except Uncle Grant; but not until they were both adults. Grant kept his secret, only revealing it to me and Becca after Wes's death. He agonized that he should have insisted Wesley get professional help but none of us had understood what demons he'd been fighting or how much they gnawed on his soul.

It was pretty ironic and very sad that a child from a physically abusive alcoholic father was further abused in a different way by the doctor he should have been able to trust. I knew he had struggled with self-esteem as a teenager but never understood why. Girls chased after him. He was an extremely handsome young man with an exuberant personality when hanging with friends. But he never let anyone get too close. Probably because he feared they might see the darkness he struggled against.

I think that's probably why he encouraged everyone to look up, to find the light, and to try and view the positive in all things. If there was a lesson, a purpose to his dying for me, I guess that must have been it. I try not to take anyone for granted now. I try not to waste time on petty arguments it just isn't worth it. Life is too short and it is meant for living, not brooding. I guess that's why I regret my staleness over the past few years, it is so unlike me or so unlike the person I used to be. I feel I have wasted so much time, but maybe it wasn't wasted, maybe it was my "cocoon time," my time of growth.

# Let's Pretend

November 7

Our little white farmhouse was nestled into the fold of a mountainside about half way to the top. A small, friendly creek ran behind and a dusty dirt road had been cut into the hillside above our front yard. All together we owned about thirty acres with most of the acreage lying above the road. Surrounding the house was about five acres of fairly flat land, and in spite of my father's drinking, not all of my memories from there are bad.

I can remember running out onto the front porch on early spring mornings with the concrete cold beneath my bare feet. The ground would still be damp with dew and the air would shimmer with a hint of moisture in the early morning sunlight. Birds would sing and the chickens would squawk and all would seem right with the world. It was the most peaceful place on God's earth as long as my father was behaving himself.

When my father had built our home, he had planted an orchard on one side of the house with a variety of apple trees and some pear trees. He later added blackberry vines to the orchard and we had two cherry trees in the front yard. Momma kept a small strawberry patch in her vegetable garden so we always had plenty of fresh fruit in the summer and fall with plenty to preserve for winter jams and jellies. The smokehouse, with its stash of cured ham and slabs of bacon within easy reach, was on the opposite side of the house, along with the chicken coop and the pig pens. We always had plenty of fresh eggs and fresh chickens for Sunday dinners along with a hog or two fattening in summer for a late fall butchering so there would be smoked ham for Christmas. The chop block and woodpile were nearby and convenient when a freshly butchered chicken was needed, and close enough to the house on cold winter days when wood was needed for heating or for momma's wood cook stove, which she still preferred using over the modern bottled gas one Daddy had bought her.

The pig pens were far enough away from the house to lessen the impact of their smell on hot summer days, and still farther away was the barn. It was built partially into the hillside at the far end of our lower pasture with an open walkway in front that allowed fresh air to move through, while still protected from the elements by the covered hay loft above. There were four stalls and a corncrib to store shucked corn that, along with the hay stored overhead, fed the farm animals in winter. The hay loft was reached by a ladder at the end of the walkway, and while my siblings ensured me the hay loft was a good place to play, I didn't spend much time alone at the barn. It was dark and frequented by black snakes who fed on the mice and rats that came to try and steal the corn. I was so terrified of snakes, of their near silent approaches, so that coming up on one was always a shock. I preferred to keep my distance from the barn unless accompanied.

On the far end of the barn, once you passed through the walkway, was a rickety gate that led to my mom's vegetable garden. She grew things like snap peas, green beans, lettuce and onions, with patches of rhubarb at the end of the rows for rhubarb dumplings and pies. There were usually also hills of popcorn stalks—a favorite treat—and squash and pumpkin for fall. Most other crops Daddy grew in large quantity; some were cash crops, so he planted them in the upper fields, above the upper pastures where the cows grazed in the summertime. As they grazed, they meandered slowly along with their tails swishing as they walked, and over the years they had cut crosswise slanting trails along the sloping hillside. As a child, I ran along these trails playing with my cousins or my own make believe games, or more frequently, carrying canning jars of ice water to my father and Uncle Grant as they worked the upper fields.

At the very top of the hillside, above the pasture and the upper planting fields were the hayfields. Here, the wind flowed over the alfalfa grass and sweet clover in an almost constant peaceful rhythm, and when you looked out at the surrounding mountaintops, it was as if you could see forever. A good hay crop was important to feed the animals in winter and Daddy also raised a large corn crop. And in the fall after the ears of corn had been pulled and only the skeletal stalks remained, we would gather these into *fodder shocks* to also be used as animal food in the cold winter months ahead.

I remember standing there in the cornfield with Becca and Wesley as they tied up the shocks looking down at our little farmhouse. It seemed sturdy and inviting as smoke puffed from the chimneys and the lighted windows beckoned with a promise of the warmth inside. It made me feel good deep inside, there with my siblings, knowing the crops were stored to feed us through the winter. We had coal and wood to heat our home, and maybe if I was a really, really good girl, daddy wouldn't drink again for a long, long time.

My childhood wasn't unbearably awful: I suffered no molestation, I wasn't locked in a dark closet all alone for hours on end, and there was no hunger, no lack of medical care. In fact, my parents were very modern in that we actually saw a pediatrician for regular physicals and childhood sicknesses. Of course in hindsight, perhaps that wasn't a good thing, but like any good parent, they thought they were doing what was best for their children and, at that time in our area, most children were lucky if they ever saw the local family doctor, even when extremely ill, much less an actual pediatrician.

I was an adult before I heard the term "dysfunctional family" but I knew we weren't like other families. After all, Ward Cleaver was tough but he didn't beat his boys, and Ben Cartwright was always there when his sons needed him; he wasn't lying semi-comatose in a drunken stupor on the couch. Even Fred Flintstone and Darren Stevens were family men. But in our house, we lived with the knowledge of being different. We acknowledged that we worked harder than most of the children we went to school with, but we avoided the real facts of living with the shame and uncertainty of never knowing if you could count on Daddy to be there when you needed him or not; of never knowing if he would be nice to your friends or embarrass you in front of them. Always afraid others would see his drunkenness and the shame would fall on you.

To escape the reality, I created a pretend family who lived in our backyard. I liked visiting them. They were just like us but their daddy didn't drink. He didn't yell and cuss when he thought they weren't working hard enough. He didn't call them stupid or make them feel small in front of other children. I also invented a make-believe twin sister. We looked alike—identical twins—so we dressed alike too. Whenever I wanted to I could pretend to be her because she was the strong one. Things didn't upset her or frighten her as much as they did me and she would always remind me that we were just as good as everybody else, no matter what our daddy said or did. She gave me the support I needed to get through the hard times as well as someone I could look out for; someone who needed me. It helped me cope to feel I shared the fears with her, and if things got too bad inside the house, we would go and visit that other family in the backyard. They were really poor so we would bring them food since there was always plenty of food in our house. It made us feel better to think that while their daddy didn't drink, he still didn't take good care of them because they never had enough to eat. Our daddy might've been a drunk, but he made sure we had plenty of food along with fresh milk and eggs to grow big and strong.

I remember worrying about that pretend family when we moved away from the farm. I don't know when I finally gave up my twin; it seems she was a part of me for a long time. Pretend friends were safer as they understood about your old man being a drunk and they weren't going to gossip about it to others.

Surprised that anyone would be coming to the studio so early, Tess hurried to the front of the store at the sound of the door chime. "Good morning, how can I help you?" she asked the back of the tall, blond haired man that stood in the reception area.

The man turned with a smile and she realized it was Bob Kirkenbaum. "Good morning!" He smiled, showing his perfectly symmetrical teeth. "It's nice to see you again. I've been meaning to stop by ever since I heard about Ross being in the hospital." She noted the crinkles at the corners of his eyes and the way his shirt pulled tight over his broad shoulders as he moved. "Although I'm sure things are fine in your capable hands," he added.

Tess smiled. "Things are good. A little hectic of course, but we seem to be running smoothly at the moment." She gestured to a stack of papers on the counter. "Local Businessman has Surgery in the Hospital's New Cardiology Department," the headline proclaimed. "That story in the paper has brought in a lot of business!" she said.

He tilted his head to the side. "Well then, I don't suppose you'd be interested in taking on a new project, would you?" he asked with a grin, raising his eyebrows in challenge.

She chuckled, smiling broadly. "As Grant always says, 'you can't make hay when the sun don't shine,' or something like that, but anyway I'm not the kind to run from work." Giving herself a mental shake as she realized she was almost flirting with him, she composed her face and cleared her throat. "Does your mom have another fashion show coming up?"

He shook his head. "No, that's not why I'm here." He paced to the far side of the small reception area and then turned back to face her, hands tucked into the pockets of the khakis he wore as he rocked back onto his heels. "I watched the video you produced with my mom yesterday. You did the edits and finalization of this one on your own didn't you? No input from Ross, right?"

"Ouch, does it show?"

He shook his head and then smiled. "It shows, but not in a negative way. We both really liked your work. It's as good as anything we've gotten from the studio before, but it's different, softer, more pleasing to watch. There are subtle changes that we both really liked. Only after we'd watched it and discussed how much we liked it did it occur to us that with Ross having been in the hospital and now out recuperating, you must've done all the edits yourself."

She felt her cheeks grow warm, pleased at his words. "That's a relief! I was really hesitant in tackling it on my own. Your mom has been working with Ross for a long time. They're friends and he knows her preferences. But I knew she needed the footage for her last minute holiday promotions."

He reached into his jacket pocket and pulled out a folded sheet of paper, which he handed to her. "We liked it so much. Here's a purchase order for several more copies." He smiled at the surprise on her face when she saw the size of the order. "But that's not the only reason I stopped by. I really do have a business proposition

I want to discuss with you." Grinning mischievously he added, "Is now a good time, or should I see Gina for an appointment?"

*Touché*, she thought, remembering her words to him at their initial meeting. She quickly turned away, stuffing her urge to laugh deep inside. Pretending indifference, she smoothed the purchase order as she reached for an order form. "Tell you what, just let me write up this order for one of the girls to process and we'll talk, if that's okay. Or are you in a rush?" She glanced back at him, deliberately keeping her expression bland, though curiosity was stirring inside her.

"Nope, that'll be fine." He removed his outer winter jacket and hung it on the rack by the door, then made himself at home on one of the soft leather chairs, his hand reaching for a copy of the paper.

As she attached the purchase order to the order form and typed the order into the computer system, she wondered what he did for a living that he didn't need to rush off to work. Hastily scrawling the words "rush reorder" on a sticky pad to leave in the order "intake" box, she decided he must be involved in his mother's business somehow since he'd brought the purchase order in.

Walking back to the front, she spoke in her most professional voice, "The store doesn't actually open for another forty-five minutes, so we shouldn't be disturbed out here, but why don't we use Ross's office in the back, just in case?" He rose to follow her and as they moved down the narrow hallway past the cubicles where viewings were held, she became aware that his shadow loomed over her, bringing her a moment of unease. Maybe she should have talked with him out front instead of taking him all the way to the back. The store suddenly seemed very empty and quiet, and he was after all a virtual stranger. Seating him in Ross's office, she asked if he'd like a cup of coffee. "It's fresh; I made it just before you arrived."

He accepted, asking for cream, no sugar. She took deep breaths in an attempt to calm her nervousness as she filled a cup for each of them, adding cream and sugar to her own. As she passed by the rear door, she spotted Gina's car pulling in and breathed a sigh of relief. Even though she realized she felt safe from physical harm, something still made her nervous and uneasy being alone with Bob Kirkenbaum. Having regained her composure, she handed him his coffee and took a seat at Ross's desk; her mind clear and ready to hear what he had to say.

By the time he'd finished outlining his proposal, Tess's mind was churning with ideas. She hadn't realized that he owned one of the most prestigious styling salons in the area as well as his mother's modeling studio. Both had originally been his mother's businesses, but he had owned interest in them for many years. He had an MBA in business administration and a BA in marketing so, he had explained, a couple of years ago, his mother had decided she wanted to slow down and devote her time strictly to coaching, so she'd turned controlling interest in both businesses over to him.

"I own several franchised businesses now as well, but at that time, I was working in DC, so I was glad to give up the commute." He shrugged. "I had some ideas for the businesses and they worked, both businesses are doing better than ever and my franchises are doing well too, so the risks have been worth it."

Tess knew there was a lot more to it than that, including a lot of hard work, long hours, and days with little return on investment that he wasn't discussing. She admired the fact that he had been willing to put in the time and take the chance of giving up a steady paycheck for the uncertainty of running day-to-day businesses and wondered if she would have been brave enough to do the same. Job security was just another illusion, but it was hard to give up all the same.

As they talked, she learned the background of Ross's number one customer. That she had originally purchased the then small, struggling styling salon with life insurance money after her husband's drowning death in a boating accident. That her goal had been to create a relaxing environment where a woman could feel pampered and catered to. And she had succeeded. "Cherchez la Femme" was the type of salon where customers were greeted in a warm, inviting reception area with offers of wine, gourmet coffee, or sparkling spring water. Cheese was served on marble cheese boards along with a tray of exotic fruits like kiwi, mango and papaya. Decorated in restful shades of blue and green, with lots of towering live plants and soft soothing music, the woman was catered to throughout the entire experience, so in spite of the high dollar price tag attached, getting an appointment at the shop required calling sometimes weeks in advance.

"Mom was a child model and she grew up with the dream of being a modeling coach, so when the salon took off, she branched out. By then, she had a long list of regular customers who were happy to send their children to her classes and soon, the second business was booming too." Bob shook his head, smiling as he thought of his mother. "She had never worked outside the home since she and dad had married, but her natural business skills were phenomenal." He drained the remaining dregs from his coffee cup and went on to explain the purpose for his visit. Basically, he wanted to branch out and use the experience of his mother's two businesses combined with the photography studio skills to create a total photographic experience, either for actual models or just those who wanted some truly dynamic photos of themselves such as engagement or graduation photos or even glamour shots for women including moms-to-be to be or parents with newborns. "With digital photography, we have so many more options. We could do outdoor settings as well as in the studio with props and retouching for perfection, and we could utilize old costumes and props from the modeling studio such as boas and tutus or cowboy hats and boots. We could add a complete makeup and hair styling package provided by my staff at the salon. With digital, you can take many more shots to get just the perfect one. And we could also do all the new artsy trends such as extreme close ups, and soft focus; with the right photographer we could give people a true photographic experience. And we could get additional business doing a complete portfolio for the models from mom's studio, giving them the hair and makeup along with extra props for inspiration." Caught up in his excitement he leaned forward as he talked and Tess found herself leaning towards him, caught up in his words as well.

"Of course I thought of using Posterity for the photography, Mom is Ross's number one fan, and after meeting you at the fashion show, I knew you were as dedicated as he is." He smiled. "I took the liberty of having my attorney draw up the draft of the proposal. It outlines the financial details and responsibilities. I think they've come up with a proposal that will be fair to everyone. It's in my car. I'll be happy to leave it for you to review if you want to look it over. I really think this is a homerun for everyone involved."

Silently, Tess agreed, and she wondered if he'd found Ross's illness an opportune time to present the idea, feeling she might be more agreeable to the idea than her boss was. Ross was a shrewd businessman, but he was somewhat stuck with the traditional style of family photography; everyone in their Sunday best seated together. Nothing truly personal like Bob was proposing. And while they'd added digital photography, Ross still relied on the tried and true. She'd been trying to get Ross to add options for the more personal type sessions to the studio for quite some time.

People, and especially women, loved having photos that were a little unique, or that showcased their favorite hobbies or the great outdoors. Women also loved having shots that made them look better than real life like models. They purchased photos like these as gifts for spouses or lovers, or even just for the pleasure of doing a fun photo session and feeling like a model for the day. And what new mother didn't want unique special photos of their little one? With expectancy photos becoming more popular, showing the beauty of a mother in waiting, it really was the perfect time to jump onboard the wave. But Ross had always been hesitant, wary of change, wary of the hassles involved with extensive retouching, of finding a stylist, of using extensive costumes and props, distrustful of creating a studio within a studio for that type of work, distrustful of the ease of digital photography and how it could fit into his business, and of course, wary of the hassle of finding the right photographer since this type of work required spending a lot more time with the client, of being able to quickly get a sense of their personality while putting them at ease and finding just the right setting and the right angle, and the best poses, all of which would require a great deal of patience. Ross was old school, utilizing the old traditional poses and stiff back grounds. As much as he embraced technology in his editing equipment, he was still stubborn about too much change too quickly.

"Well, Bob, I think you have a great idea." She hardly noticed how easily his first name came to her lips, or how relaxed she now felt in his company after her earlier nervousness. "But, you do realize I'm just an employee? I don't have the authority to enter into a binding contract for something like this. And with Ross's recovery, I'm not sure it's the best time to approach him about making a change like this. I'll admit, you've eliminated most of the objections he's had when I've brought up similar ideas in the past," she ruminated aloud before noticing the wide smile on his face at her words. She had given away the fact that she'd thought of doing something similar in the past.

"Then don't tell him." He held up his hand to stop her words of protest. "I mean, don't tell him right away." He settled himself more comfortably in the chair, crossing his long legs at the ankles. His loafers rocking side to side as he spoke, "I realize you don't have the authority to sign a contract, but just look it over. If you think the profit divisions are fair, well, then let's give it a trial run. If it takes off like I think it's going to, he'll come around when he sees the profit figures. If it flops, you can wait and tell him when he's fully recovered."

Her mind churned. His words made sense even if it meant taking a risk, and it was the perfect time to add such a venture; people would flock to have photos taken in time for Christmas. But this wasn't her business; did she dare take such a risk without her boss's authority?

Bob must've seen her wavering expression because he smiled broadly and added, "Remember, I have a degree in marketing. I can make it fly!"

She couldn't help smiling in return; her mind racing with ideas at the challenge. "I believe you. If anyone can do it, you can!" She sighed, "But you realize, I'd have to find space to dedicate just to this venture, and I'd probably need to hire another photographer." She chewed at her lower lip absently. "I realize we would need to get this in the works quickly, but can I take a little time to think it over?"

He nodded. "Sure, I want you to take a little time and think it over. I'll run out and bring the contract in and you can review that as well."

As he headed to the front, Tess fell back into her chair with a nervous sigh, but before she could gather her wits Gina came flying into the room. "I wanna do it, Tess! Please say we're gonna do it! Don't be mad, I couldn't help but overhear, and I wanna go for it. I wanna be the photographer; I know I could be great. I have lots of patience and a good eye and I've done glamour shots before when they were all the rage. I know with practice I could be really good." The younger woman was bouncing with excitement, hands clutched under her chin.

Tess chuckled. "Whoa, slow down. I can't make a decision that fast! Besides, don't you think Ross will skin me alive and feed me to stray dogs if I take a chance like this with his business?"

"Why should he?" Gina reasoned. "After all, his business wouldn't be functioning at all right now if it wasn't for you. I say go for it like the man said. When the money starts rolling in he'll see the wisdom in it."

Bob popped back into the room just then, extending a manila envelope to Tess. "Here's the contract for your review." Tess made the brief introductions, hoping the younger woman would keep her enthusiasm to herself.

"You know," Bob added as he turned to go, "if this thing takes off, we could always rent more space here in the complex." At her startled expression he grinned and held up his hand. "But you're right, that's for the future. For now, just look these over. I'll stop by again in a couple of days and see what you've decided."

Picking up the contract after he'd gone Tess glanced through it quickly. "Gina, can you hold down the fort for a bit here? I need to drop off the payroll figures for Uncle Grant anyway and I think I'll have him take a look at this contract while I'm there."

The younger woman nodded, smiling eagerly. "You got it boss!"

# A Greater Whole

November 8

It seems this writing has become a necessary part of my existence, like breathing or eating. I don't have to do it every day but I find that I can't go too long without another "fix." It's annoying and frightening and yet exhilarating to feel that way because if I need it, then it must be working; I must be making progress, right? It feels as if I am finding myself within my own past, within my own thoughts and words. Writing it all down has helped me define just who I am. It is a very overwhelming feeling to suddenly have a truer sense of my own identity. It gives a feeling of wholeness, of oneness, if that makes sense. It also allows me to see myself not just individually but as a part of a greater whole, a puzzle piece that fits into the overall pattern of existence. In spite of the worries and financial struggles over not having enough money (for it seems there's never enough), lately in the mornings I step out into the brisk fall air and I see God's sun shining through the trees, lifting the moisture up from the earth and I take a deep breath of the cool, damp morning air and I feel such joy—joy in living, joy in my children and the love I feel for them, joy in just "being." Perhaps that is enough, just to exist and to have the intelligence to appreciate it.

I went back and read all that I have written and I realized that while my original intention had been to progress chronologically, I have been bouncing around a lot. It seems that when the memories start coming, they don't come in any particular order. I also noticed that I had never explained how Uncle Grant came to live with us, and truthfully, I don't really know how it happened in the beginning, but I do know why. Grant was the youngest of my grandparent's children, born just sixteen months before my parents were married. Grandpa was in his seventies by then and his big brother, my dad, seemed more of a father figure to him. Both Momma and Daddy spoiled him during the months while they were still living with my grandparents. I guess they were practicing for their own baby. He was barely three when Becca was born and Momma just always treated him like another one of her own. So I guess as he grew and time passed, it just felt natural to him to spend more and more time at our house.

Momma always said Grant was God's wedding gift to her. She always depended on him; we all did when we were younger. And Grant was just our natural leader, taking the brunt of daddy's anger from the rest of us whenever he could. As he grew to be a man, Momma knew she could always depend on him to keep the farm going when Daddy was on a drunken spree. Grant reminds me of Grandpa, even though Daddy mostly raised him, just in the way that he never has much to say. I like to tease him and tell him that he might have Grandpa's name, but I got his special healing powers.

Grandpa was known as a healer in our small community and was said to have the power of goodness. His brother, my great uncle John, was said to have powers as well, but his were of darkness and evil. Neighbors would swear Uncle John put a curse or cast a spell on their cows or other livestock and they would call Grandpa to come and remove it.

Grandpa knew the medicinal qualities of the mountain herbs and plants and where to find them growing in the woods. He knew how to dry them and how to turn them into salve or brew them into teas. He also knew a lot about anatomy although he basically had no formal education; he had taught himself. So these things when added to the fact that he had a natural way with animals—being able to calm them so that they never minded his touch—combined with his strong belief in the power of prayer and faith, made it easy to for him to work with a sick animal. However, his clannish, backwards mountain neighbors believed there was more magic than science in his healing administrations.

I can't say I really knew him very well as I was only eight when he died. But I think if he possessed any power, it was the power of goodness, of God's love and compassion, and of human kindness. He was nearly one hundred when he died, and he practiced what medical journals preach today for longevity: a healthy diet and exercise. He carried a cane when he walked, but I don't think he actually used it much. In fact, he had a collection of canes including many beautiful store bought ones, but my favorites were the handmade ones that he had whittled and smoothed with his own hands from gnarled walking sticks. I remember watching as he sat on the front porch of their tiny farmhouse as his hands smoothed and polished his canes. I think he carried them more as a symbol of wisdom and dignity than for any practical use.

Grandpa was named Grant after Ulysses S. Grant, not that his relatives had fought for the North in the War Between the States. They were Southerners through and through. Too poor to own slaves, and too far back in the sticks to even truly understand what the war was all about; they just knew the South had called them to arms and they fought to protect their land and their families. My great grandma simply thought Grant made a strong sounding name for a man, and when my grandpa was born, she was said to have described him as the runt of the litter. It was said that she chose the name Grant because she decided he would need a strong sounding name to carry him through life. But who knows, maybe she was a unionist at heart. Uncle Grant was named after Grandpa. I've always thought it was a strong name.

I remember my grandpa as a small framed man with finely boned hands and a mustache that bounced when he talked. He was bald on top and had short tufts of hair along the sides of his head. His general form of dress was bibbed overalls and flannel shirts and I remember the combination of crisp denim and soft flannel against my cheek when he hugged me. He would smell of lava soap and either Teaberry or Juicy Fruit gum; he'd given up chewing tobacco and switched to chewing gum in his eighties, so I only remember him with the fresh smell of gum in his bib pocket.

After giving me a piece of *Grandpa's gum* which was how he always described it, he would snuggle me close and smooth his hands over my long hair in a caressing, gentle motion, much like I had seen him soothe a sick animal or gently polish his canes. Then we would sit quietly side by side on the old metal glider that sat on their front porch. Occasionally, his hand would reach out to once again stroke my hair as his eyes roamed the horizon, his thoughts far away. Sometimes he would make me promise that I would never cut my long hair, and I always agreed; I would have promised Grandpa anything.

In the fall when the apples were ripe, he'd bring several onto the porch with us and he would peel and core them with his pocket knife for us to share. He'd had all of his teeth pulled and dentures made years before, but he never got used to wearing the dentures and they now spent all their time in a teacup in the cupboard. His gums had toughened over the years and he could eat just about anything he wanted, so he never bothered wearing them.

We seldom talked; Grandpa wasn't one for idle chatter and always listened more than he talked. He was greatly respected in the community for his wisdom and even then modern veterinarians or new mothers with colicky newborns would seek out his advice or ask for remedies to try. And in spite of our silences, I feel that Grandpa taught me a lot during our visits. I was one of his few grandchildren that was content to just sit with him. Most, in typical childlike fashion, wanted to be up and running, playing and laughing. With cousins scattered to several states by then, it wasn't often that I saw some of them, so I felt shy around my more "sophisticated" city cousins, and then, as now, I wasn't really comfortable in crowds. I was fortunate in that I saw grandpa more often than most of my cousins did since we lived just over the mountain, and I cherished the opportunity to sit with him and stare out at the distant blue horizon of the surrounding mountains.

I knew my grandma even less well than I knew my grandpa even though she lived for almost twenty years after his death. She was very grandmotherly in many ways, with a big soft bosom to give comforting hugs, but there was bad blood between her and my mom, and sometimes she would be upset with both my parents, usually over my father's drinking. Sometimes after giving you a big hug, she would try to get you to reveal things you'd overheard or had been told not to talk about, which always made me uncomfortable. Until my father's death, I would pretend to be too shy to speak up whenever she tried to get me to discuss something. I would bury my face in her bosom and mumble a reply that could be taken any way she chose.

In a small community there are always rumors swirling and people who believe the worst about others and there were those who believed my grandmother held the powers of darkness, as my great uncle John had supposedly possessed. It was rumored that only the power of my grandfather's goodness held her in check through the years. For me, I am certain that any powers of goodness and light come from God, and any miracles are through God's grace. But perhaps, there is also a power of darkness and it too will perform dark miracles for us if we reach for it and if we choose to believe in it. I have never believed my grandmother possessed any evil beliefs. Over the years, I have come to believe that maybe grandma wanted some people to believe she had these powers, people that she didn't like or that had done her wrong in some way. But I have actually come to feel sorry for my grandmother and the tough life she lived. I am sure she had a very discontented life, married to a much older man, with no money for the frills and extras that a young woman craves. Instead, there was just one baby after another, and then the children grew quickly and left her behind. I think the rumor of possessing dark powers just added a spark of excitement to an otherwise somewhat lonely life.

If anything, I believe her power came from the power of suggestion. People will often do what we want if we just repeat the suggestion often enough, and an intelligent woman like my grandma could insult you while making it sound like a compliment. A trait I have actually utilized myself. Strong willed with an equally strong work ethic, I realize my own work ethic and inner strength as a woman probably have their roots with her as well as with my own mother.

After both my grandpa and daddy had passed away, I didn't see grandma very often over the years. Life was never the same once we had left the farm and my Virginia cousins and grandparents behind. And in spite of the harshness of my early life, those years always brought great security and I had always felt surrounded by love.

Considering the chaos of our home during the final years of Daddy's life, it's amazing that I would feel that way. But from my siblings, momma, grandpa, grandma, cousins, aunts and uncles, and even my daddy, everyone always made me feel special, had always told me I was a special little girl. I think all of this love taught me to reach for the light, for the goodness in everything, because it has always been there like a blanket, a shield from the darkness, if I only remember to look for it.

Life has a bright side and a dark side
For the world of relativity
Is composed of light and shadows.
If you permit your thoughts
To dwell on evil
You yourself will become ugly.
Look only for the good
In everything,
That you absorb the
Quality of beauty.

From the sayings of:
Paramahansa Yogananda

# A New Adventure

Bob smiled a greeting to Tess as he entered the shop the next morning, the warmth of her return smile giving him hope that she'd agreed to his proposal. "Good morning." He jiggled the bakery bag he held. "I hope you're not one of those women who diet all the time, cause I brought pastries."

Tess laughed. "Hasn't your mother taught you to never question a woman about her diet?"

He shrugged, grinning sheepishly. "Actually, I have a weakness for Bavarian cream and I was hoping you'd join me so I wouldn't feel so guilty making a pig of myself."

Tess found herself grinning back at him. "Well, truthfully, I'm a very poor dieter, and I happen to love Bavarian cream. Come on back to Ross's office and I'll get the coffee, it's fresh."

"Make mine with—"

She interrupted. "I know, just a touch of cream."

He smiled as he tore sheets of paper towel from the roll he found on top of a file cabinet. He hoped her good mood was a positive sign as well.

"Here we are." Carefully placing his coffee in front of him, she sat behind the desk in Ross's chair. "Oooh, these look good!" As she bit into the chocolate frosted richness of the doughnut, the thick cream squeezed out from the sides and she greedily slurped it up, licking the stickiness from her fingers as well. Glancing up she caught Bob watching her, an amused expression on his face. Embarrassed, she took a gulp of coffee, shrugging as she told him, "I warned you I loved these things!"

He grinned before biting into his own pastry and she was pleased to see he was an even bigger glutton than she was, taking half the donut in one bite. When he licked at the corners of his mouth, she laughed. It was impossible to eat the gooey confections with any semblance of dignity.

After finishing off her pastry, Tess held up a hand to stop him from placing a second one in front of her. "Enough, I've just eaten half of my calorie allotment for the day!"

He shrugged. "You're so tiny I don't think a second pastry is going to ruin your figure."

*What figure?* she thought, wiping her hands on a fresh paper towel; she knew he was just being nice, like a salesman. After all, he was trying to sell her on his idea and she knew how full of it salesmen were, right? Fleetingly, Troy's image flashed through her mind and she immediately sobered, reminding herself that this was just a business meeting, nothing more. Pushing her hair back from her face, she again sat behind the desk and folded her hands in her lap, waiting for him to begin.

Noticing the sudden change in her mood, Bob wondered what had caused it. Had his remark about her figure been too personal? Probably, but he thought he'd just been stating the obvious; she was small framed and if there was any extra fat on her he could see no sign of it. But maybe his remark could be construed as sexist and he didn't want her to think he didn't take her seriously just because she was a woman. In fact, he knew from his own mother just what a strong woman was capable of and he thought Tess Quinlan was cut from the same material.

Jokingly, he shoved the bag of pastries to the side. "You're right! No more for me either or I'll lose my boyish figure for sure!" He hoped his silly remark would clear the air, but Tess's expression remained the same. "You know, the older I get the harder I find it is to work these things off. Of course I'm not as enthused about working out as I used to be."

"Do you go to the gym?" she asked politely.

He shook his head. "I made a small gym in the space over my garage at home. I'm not much for public gyms. What about you, do you belong to a gym?"

Shaking her head, Tess replied, "No, I can't afford the membership, but I do try to work out at home a few days each week. I like the energy boost it gives me, and with three kids I need all the energy I can get."

He smiled. "Three kids, you are a busy woman!" She finally smiled and he asked her their ages, surprised to find that she had teenagers; she looked too young for that, but he didn't pry. The remarks on her weight had already caused him enough trouble and his mom would truly thump him on the head if he asked a woman about her age.

Seeing she was more relaxed after discussing her children, he leaned back in his chair and asked, "Did you look over the proposal? Have you reached a decision?"

Tess looked down at her hands, which were nervously intertwined in her lap. "I did, and I talked to everyone seeking advice. I showed Grant the proposal, I called my sister, I talked it over with my kids and I even spoke to Becky, Ross's wife."

"And?" he asked when she paused. Suddenly, her answer was very important. There were other studios in town, several that already offered similar services, and he knew he could approach them but he knew that Posterity was one of the most respected and suddenly, he very much wanted to work with Tess, to see her blossom as the project became a success.

She smiled, meeting his gaze head on. "Everyone told me it was a great idea, and that it sounded like an enjoyable project. Even Becky thought it sounded like a good idea and she told me the studio was in my hands so I had to make my own decisions. Gina is ecstatic at the idea and practically begged me for the opportunity to be our photographer. So…" She paused, nibbling at her lower lip. "My answer is yes, let's give it a trial period and see what happens."

He jumped from his chair so quickly she was startled. "Great! It's gonna bring in a lot of business, just wait and see." He held his hand out and pumped hers enthusiastically.

Tess couldn't help grinning at his enthusiasm. "How about a trial period running through Valentine's Day? By that time, Ross should be back at work and he can decide if he wants to make it permanent or not."

Bob nodded as she spoke. "That sounds like a great plan to me. How long before you're ready to get started?" he asked as he settled back into his chair.

They discussed logistics, bouncing ideas back and forth on how they could make things move along as quickly as possible. Tess ruminated out loud about the rearranging she would need to do and the things she could put in storage in order to make space, her eyes lighting up with enthusiasm as she talked. "I think we should work by appointment only, we keep pretty flexible hours anyway, and for photos like these you don't want anyone to feel pressured or stressed. Gina is willing to be flexible with her schedule, she's eager to have this opportunity."

Bob watched her face as she talked, secretly smiling to himself as he watched her run with the project as he had known she would once she made the decision to give it a try. He could still sense some hesitancy behind the enthusiasm, but that was understandable, given her position. "How about we aim to try and open here?" He pointed to the calendar to the Monday that was only ten days away. "I've got ads and marketing ideas ready to roll and I'll put fliers up at the salon and at the modeling studio. I'm working on doing a commercial for the local cable channel as well; we can do that cheaply since we can shoot the footage ourselves." His enthusiasm matched hers and he rambled on, wanting to reassure her that he was prepared to run with this project as well. "I even have a hair dresser who's fresh out of school. She's really talented with makeup and she's eager to make a name for herself so she'll be willing to be flexible with her time as well." He tapped a finger against the corner of the desk and she could almost see the wheels turning inside his head. "Like Gina, she's single and thrilled to be given this opportunity. I think they'll make a good pair."

Each fueled the other's fire as the ideas bounced back and forth and they finished the pot of coffee as they filled legal pads with notes and tossed ideas and worked out details between them. They were both eager for the project to be a success so they needed to hit the ground running, with no loose ends or minor details left undone to slow things down. The morning flew by and suddenly, Gina was tapping at the door, reminding them that it was lunch time.

Stunned, Tess glanced at her watch. "I can't believe it's noon already!" She rose and stretched out the kinks in her back that were letting her know just how much time she'd spent in the chair.

Bob stood as well. "Let me buy you lunch, we can have a mini celebration." He watched her face as he spoke and could immediately sense a withdrawal, a shutting down as she started to shake her head no. Before she could verbalize her refusal, he turned to the younger woman. "Gina, would you like to join us for lunch to celebrate your new position?"

Gina whooped for joy. "Yes sir! Sounds great! Where we going?"

Grinning, he turned back to Tess, who finally nodded her agreement. He didn't know who or what had made her so gun shy around men, but someone must've hurt her pretty badly in the past. She seemed to only be comfortable around him as long as they were discussing business. If the atmosphere even hinted at anything personal, such as lunch, he could sense her withdrawal as she pulled back into her shell.

# The Beginning

November 11

My parents met through mutual friends and dated only a short while before they wed. Daddy had just returned from the war and Momma thought he was very handsome in his uniform. He was a sharp dresser and whenever he came calling if he wasn't wearing his uniform he always wore a suit, and often a hat as well. Being six years older than Momma, she found him worldly and she sat fascinated as he spoke of his war experiences and of the people he'd met in France and England. Being a *mountain girl* she'd never left the shelter of the hills, traveling no farther than neighboring West Virginia to visit relatives in her entire life. Reading was her escape and to hear him talk of actually being in places she'd only read about or heard about from news stories was very exciting, so he easily swept her off of her feet.

Of course, daddy was equally smitten with her. She was a petite young woman of eighteen with thick black, wavy hair hanging to her shoulders, with hazel green Irish eyes and a naturally olive complexion. Standing just over five feet tall, she weighed less than a hundred pounds and yet curved in all the right places. After the horrors he'd witnessed in the war, I am sure her sweetness and her innocence combined with her beauty swept him off his feet as well.

They married in early fall in a brief ceremony conducted at a minister's home, just across the state line in Kentucky. Afterwards, he took her for a steak dinner at the only restaurant in the small town, just down the street from the minister's house. Being shy and not used to eating in public, she allowed him to cut her steak for her and admired his self-assurance as he told her not to be embarrassed because people were just people the world over and everyone had to eat. But in her nervousness she found it impossible to eat much of her meal and finally he had it wrapped for them to take with them.

They had someone to give them a ride back to the top of the mountain above my grandparents' house, but had to walk the final mile and a half along a rutted wagon road that gave the only access to the farm. I've often heard Momma speak of that walk in the cool autumn air. A full moon was rising across the mountaintops, and the air was so sharp and clear it seemed almost as if she could reach up and touch it. The acorns were thick underfoot and it was impossible to take a step without crunching them, which made walking difficult and she clutched Daddy's hand tightly. Newly married with Daddy's hand holding hers and the gentle autumn breeze whispering through her hair, the world must have seemed almost perfect at that moment.

A heavy frost fell that night and Grandpa predicted a long, hard winter ahead, and his predictions turned out to be true. But Grandma was an industrious woman and their table was never lacking. Nervous at meeting her new husband's large, boisterous family, she found herself overwhelmed by the differences when compared to her own. Daddy's family yelled and shouted and the many boys punched and tussled with one another. Her own family was quiet and peaceful except when Pappy and her brothers were making music. But in spite of these things, Momma was very happy. Grandma taught her many things about housekeeping and cooking and she learned to preserve and pickle and dry vegetables and fruits so that nothing went to waste. She helped Grandma with the quilting and the mending and in tending to Grant and Daddy's other siblings. My momma was Grandma's first daughter-in-law and she was happy to have another woman in the house since her own daughters were still small.

Within a short time, Daddy had purchased land from a neighbor only a few miles from his parents' farm and, in the spring, he started building their house. By the time Becca was born the following winter, they had settled into their new home. Her birth was a cause for much celebration and my daddy and his older half-brother Henry drank hot toddies and toasted mother and baby for most of the night. Henry had a wooden peg leg and as he paced around my momma's bed, his leg tapping against the hardwood floor, he tried to sing a ditty to the new baby, misquoting lyrics about daddy's little fatty.

My momma's gentle nature harbored a fiery Irish temper and she grew annoyed with his singing, not only was he getting the words to the song all mixed up, especially since her new baby was a girl, but Henry's drunkenness also upset her. In spite of the hardships of her own early childhood, she wasn't used to drunken behavior so she angrily insisted my dad remove him from the room. Later, when Henry sobered up, Momma found him to be gentle and kind and very helpful with the baby. Over the years, he became a good friend and would frequently come to do general handyman type work around the farm or to help Momma in her garden.

When I think about my father's early ambition and what a hard worker he was, I know that we could have had a very comfortable life, a happy contented life, if not for his drinking. But it was many years before his drinking got bad enough to start creating serious problems; before he started using Momma and his children as a means to vent his frustration. Daddy was a perfectionist and when fighting the demon of the drink, his anger often took over and nothing they did was ever good enough. I think this was probably an effort to cover his own shame at the failure he saw in himself when he could not control the drinking.

Momma always said he cheated them out of the best years of their marriage; the golden years when it would have been just the two of them and they could have found true closeness. Though most people never think of it in this way, I feel alcoholism is a form of suicide. It's a very slow form, but suicide all the same; one that harms not just self but everyone around you and it forces those that love you to watch as you slowly kill yourself. It leaves them hurt, bitter, angry, and feeling like a failure because the drinker chose to die rather than seek help in order to stay with them.

Tess re-read the words she had written, surprised to find that by writing them down she had given life to thoughts that had been lying dormant, only half formed inside of her mind for years, like seeds buried beneath the winter snow. The writing was like the spring sunshine that encouraged them to sprout and bloom to fullness, allowing her to decipher impressions and images that were stamped into her subconscious. Things she'd never given much thought to before, such as how pretty her mother must have been as a young woman, or how nervous and excited she must have felt on her wedding day. Suddenly, she could understand the wistfulness in her mother's voice when she had talked of that special day.

It occurred to her that maybe she'd never really taken the time to see them as people before. By writing the memories and thoughts and impressions down, it was as if she pulled them from the fog of transient thought into the light of consciousness, where with clarity she could see the past as reality and not just as a story she'd been told. It was odd to realize that *then* had been as modern to her parents as *now* was to her.

Once the tap had been turned, the memories kept pouring out, pushing and crowding each other inside of her mind like schoolchildren on a playground, each striving to be first, as if hands were raised and voices were saying pick me, pick me. It was overwhelming and yet reassuring in that it gave her a sense of continuity, of belonging to a greater whole. Smiling, she suddenly remembered how self-assured she had been as a child, certain she was the hub around which her family turned. Certainly all young children felt that way, but for her, the fantasy had lasted much longer, nearly into adolescence.

Perhaps she'd been spoiled by all of the attention, but within a very short span of time it had all changed. Her grandpa and her daddy had died within eighteen months of each other, and then it seemed as if all too swiftly, her siblings and Grant had flown the nest, either to marriages or to lives of their own. It had left her feeling so alone, abandoned almost. They had continued to love her, to let her know how important she was to them, but it hadn't been the same; she still felt as if she was the one they'd left behind.

Her siblings and Uncle Grant had always seemed to expect excellence of her, forever telling her how smart she was. She wondered if she were a disappointment to any of them. Being alone had been hard to take, so when she'd met Billy, she had clung to him, gladly marrying him to have someone to call her own. She had willingly given up dreams of college and a career. She had loved being a stay-at-home mommy and could have gone right on that way had things been different. Did any of them understand?

Becca had chosen a different course for herself, having a career of her own as a registered nurse, and of course, Wesley was gone before his life ever really got started; but they had seemed to expect more of her. She knew Uncle Grant found her to be too bossy and independent, of course that was mainly because she insisted on paying rent for the small house on his property that she used. Besides, what else could she be besides independent? Who did she have to depend on besides herself? Being independent was a matter of survival, not choice. She'd become who she had to be. Some choices were free choices, like deciding to work hard at being a good mother, or conditioning ourselves not to walk with a slouch, but you had to play the hand life dealt you and do the best you could with it. If you folded every time things came up deuces instead of aces, then you might as well let them lock you away in a padded cell right now. Of course there were times when she longed for someone else to be the strong one, to help carry the load, but that longing didn't change the reality.

With a shiver she rose to add more wood to the stove. It was better not to dwell on those thoughts so she moved to the kitchen to fill the teakettle. It had become a comforting habit once the kids were in bed or at least settled in their rooms for the night to put on her old bathrobe and snuggle into the recliner with her journal and a hot cup of cocoa and allow her mind to reminisce. She'd sat too long tonight though; it was nearly midnight, and she had work tomorrow. But her head was too full for sleep.

While she waited for the water to heat, she checked on the kids, making sure their rooms were warm enough. The nights were growing cooler and soon she would need to bring in the kerosene heater from the shed to help heat the bedrooms at the back of the house. Either that or turn on the electric furnace and she dreaded the larger electric bills that would bring.

# FORGIVE US OUR DEBTS

November 12

As I was tucking Sam into bed tonight, I remembered my own bedtime routine as a child. In spite of my mother's illness in my early years, I think one of my most cherished memories is of our bedtime ritual. After tucking me in, she would lie down beside of me and tell me a bedtime story, or sometimes, if she was really tired after a long day of gardening or canning, she would ask me to tell her a story. Some nights I would recite familiar stories, such as *The Three Bears* or her favorite, *The Little Red Hen*, but my favorite stories were ones I made up myself. They stared a character called Stinky, because she liked to play in the pigpen or the coal pile, or do all sorts of other naughty things, like sitting in mud puddles while wearing her good clothes.

This must have been at the phase of my childhood where I liked to shock adults with tales of bad stuff or the use of "not nice" words, like Stinky wallowing in the pigpen with the hogs. I would giggle when my momma would gasp and say, "*Oh my, what a bad little girl! I pity her poor momma trying to get those clothes clean.*" My Stinky stories were told strictly for the effect they had on Momma. I guess I was hoping that in comparison to Stinky, I was a really good little girl.

After our story time, Momma would recite the Lord's Prayer, line by line, "*Our Father who art in heaven,*" she would begin. And I would repeat it behind her, "*Our father who art in heaven.*" Line by line went this way, through the entire prayer. It may have been a strange, lengthy prayer for such a small child, and I didn't fully understand the words, but it was Momma's favorite prayer, and by the time I was five, I could recite the entire prayer all by myself. I still say that prayer nightly, partially because it is such a beautiful prayer, and partially because of the warm memories it conjures up of the two of us lying there in the darkness, warmed by the covers—soft, comforting quilts momma had sewn with her own hands—our voices soft and low in the night. Her older, steady voice quietly whispering the words and my childish, baby voice repeating them in return. At the end of the prayer we always added, "*And God Bless Mommie and Daddy and Becca, Wesley, Tess and Uncle Grant. And Bless Grandpa and Grandma and all of those we know and love. Forgive us for our sins and watch over us and take care of us always. In Jesus name we pray, Amen.*"

I was always comforted by the forgiveness part. I could envision all sorts of horrors as a consequence of my childish sins. I wasn't even certain, at least not a hundred percent certain, that telling stories about a little girl like Stinky might not be a sin, after all, I was at least thinking about doing those bad things in order to make them up; sometimes, the thought of squishing mud between your toes sounded like a lot of fun. So maybe my stories were filled with sins, but at least the forgiveness part protected me, just in case.

I wonder if my momma ever realized what a special gift she gave me when she taught me the Lord's Prayer? My blessings at the end of my prayer each night are still pretty much the same, and I think our prayers have been answered. I think He has always watched over me, even when I have made bad choices. The nightly ritual always gives me peace and it helps to think that I am laying all my concerns in his hands. In a world filled with change, we all need something to hold onto.

I have worked so much since my own kids were small that I sometimes wonder if they will have warm memories of their own childhoods. It has often seemed that I have so little time to give them, and yet they are the center of my life—all that I do, I do for them. I hope someday they will realize that. Our life certainly hasn't been a *Leave It to Beaver* episode. No family dinners around the table, no going to church as a family on Sunday. The kids and I attended Sunday school when they were small, but we never stayed for church. I couldn't afford the dresses to wear and Billy would get mad if I donated more money than he thought I should. He never went with us. He said people just went to church to show off their clothes and the church just wanted our money. But I'm glad I gave my children at least that much exposure to church. Now our lives are so hectic, always rushing from thing to thing. I just hope they know how much I love them. I try to share my days with them, try to be a part of their lives, but I know they are growing to the age where it's natural to push our parents out. I just hope that somehow our past connections will be enough to sustain a lasting bond.

November 14

Thinking of Momma the other night made me long to hear her voice so I pulled out a video I had done of her on one of her last birthdays. As I watched and listened, I realized how much my own voice has become like hers. When I reached puberty, with my dad being gone, I had no real male role model, so I made him a martyr, forgetting all the bad he had brought to my childhood. I vehemently denied any resemblance to my mother; I insisted I looked more like him, that I carried only a minimal amount of my mother's genes. But the truth is, I not only look more like her but I sound like her as well, and Tressa looks and sounds like us both, except for her curls. Of course, she's now at that age of denial, which I think is just a natural part of growing up for a girl. They push their mothers away and identify with their fathers as a way to learn to interact with the opposite sex. I worry about Tressa, with Billy as her role model.

Momma's early years were very hard as well and I have often wished I could have made up for that somehow. I am sure her major personality traits were formed very early by the tragedy of her mother's death to tuberculosis.

Myrtle, my maternal grandmother, was a strong willed and determined woman, with the same dark bushy brows and deep set eyes that I see staring back at me in the mirror each morning. She loved her children—Momma and my Uncle Teddy—fiercely and when she died, she left behind a legacy of love in the several sizes of clothing for them to wear as they grew that she had made for them on her deathbed. She also left beautiful handmade quilts, bedspreads, and crocheted table scarves. Uncle Teddy could remember her showing him which were to be his and which were for Momma. She also left them an inheritance of rich "bottomland" that had been left to her by her parents on their deaths.

Unfortunately, Pappy was a music-making Irishman who could forget time and place at the strum of a banjo. He picked banjo the old fashioned way, claw hammer I think it's called. He was one of the area's best and was always in demand for shindigs, barn raisings, or any other music making occasion. It has been rumored that he once boarded with the family of bluegrass great Ralph Stanley when he was a boy. Ralph grew up to be known nationwide for his music, a seller of millions of records, the county's most famous citizen, but Pappy just loved to pick.

Myrtle had brought stability back to Pappy's life after his first wife had walked away and left him with their two young sons. After Myrtle's death, he drifted aimlessly for several years lost in his grief. All that had been stable and secure in my momma's home died with Myrtle and overnight, the loving world she and Teddy had known disappeared as Pappy drifted through his days, allowing life to happen to him and to his children. Being a logger, he stayed away in the woods all week and on the weekends; it was easy to get distracted on the long walk home by a banjo tune or a harmonica's call, and once he had stopped to pick a tune, the minutes would stretch to hours while the hillsides rang with haunting tunes and foot stomping ballads that Pappy could so easily coax from his banjo.

My mother and Uncle Teddy were left with many different people during the months following my grandmother's death. Several families even asked to adopt one or the other of them, and many were in much better shape financially so they could have provided a stable, supportive home for them. But Pappy had dreams of making a home for them again so he would move them from place to place, not wanting them to grow too close to anyone, for fear they would want to stay forever. They were his last ties to Myrtle, who had been his stability and had inspired him to do more, to strive harder, and to reach for success, even when he was sure he would fail, and now she was gone.

Their little house stood empty for long periods of time, only occasionally being used by my Uncle Hank, Momma's half brother from Pappy's first marriage. He was thirteen when Myrtle died and her death left him as much an orphan as it did Momma and Teddy. She was basically the only mother he had ever known and he felt adrift without her as well. He eventually went to work in the CC camps until he was old enough to join the army. He loved his little brother and sister, but he was only a boy, so he spent much of his time with friends.

To the harsh, backward mountain folk, a house standing empty was fair game. Soon, relatives, neighbors and people presumed to be friends had stripped their home of Myrtle's possessions, even taking the clothing she had lovingly made for her children in the last few months of her life. Soon, they barely had a change of clothes or any covers for their beds. Greedy creditors even found a way to take the deed to the land that had been left to her children so that everything she had worked so hard to give them was gone.

Many years later, while my mother was visiting at a friend's house she was standing at the dresser fixing her hair when her friend told her the dresser had been Myrtle's. Momma said she lovingly touched the dresser, imagining her mother standing in front of the mirror and polishing the wood. Never had she longed for anything more than to own that dresser; she even asked to buy it and was told when they got a new one she could have it, but it was never meant to be. Momma never got the dresser. That was always such sad story to me, and I always wished I could get that dresser for momma. It was a small but significant connection to a mother she could not remember. Most people, even those that had stolen their clothing and other possessions, still tried to help by caring for them and feeding them. But this was during the Great Depression, when times were desperate and every morsel of food was difficult to come by. Before her fourth birthday, my mother had learned what it meant to be an outsider, always second best, only good enough for the hand-me-downs and the leftovers. A lesson that remained with her for life; she was always very self conscious, always worried about being a burden, always apologizing for putting others out. She never lost those feelings of inferiority.

I think the cruelest memory that she shared with me of those early years involves Pappy's family, his brother and his nephews. Momma and Teddy had been left home alone with Hank while Pappy was working one sunny spring day, but one of Hank's buddies had come by with a fishing pole and some freshly dug worms, and Hank had joined him at his favorite fishing hole. As the hours passed and he didn't return, Momma and Teddy grew hungry, and being only children they didn't think about the burden two extra mouths could be, no matter how small, so they decided to walk to their uncle's house and ask for food. They knew the way; he lived just through the woods and the trail was marked by a well worn path.

They arrived just as the family was sitting down to a meal. Pappy's brother and his wife were annoyed by their arrival. Maybe they had already fed them several times that week or maybe they were annoyed that Pappy was always leaving them alone. Whatever the reason, instead of inviting them in to eat with them, their uncle yelled at them through the open doorway and told them to go home, as one might scold a dog that comes looking for scraps. When the children didn't leave the porch, he sent his sons out and one of the boys lifted Uncle Teddy up and took him out into the yard where a new well was being dug and dropped him down inside. The digging had only recently started so the hole wasn't that deep, but it easily kept a small boy trapped inside. Laughing at their joke, the boys returned to their dinner.

Terrified by Teddy's cries when they scooped him up, Momma chased her older cousins and watched as her brother was dropped into the well. Her one clear memory of her mother's funeral was of being lifted onto someone's shoulders to watch as the coffin was lowered into the ground, so seeing Teddy in the dark, damp hole brought back the memory, and she sat at the top and screamed his name until she couldn't cry anymore, her hunger forgotten.

When their meal was finished, their uncle and cousins came and lifted Teddy from the hole. Handing each child a biscuit filled with jam, they sent them home. Still shaken by the ordeal, Momma dropped her biscuit to cling to Teddy's hand. One of her uncle's hounds quickly gobbled it up and then turned and growled at Teddy, wanting him to give up his food as well. Holding tightly to each other's hands, they ran home, sharing the remaining cold biscuit in the sanctuary of their own little house.

There were many similar episodes, though none quite so heartless, over the next few years until Pappy finally put his grief behind him and remarried for the third time when Momma was six. After three long years of never being in the same place for very long, she finally had a stable home, and while she would never fully regain her sense of security, of belonging that had left her when Myrtle had died, her life had stability again. And her new stepmother soon gave her the gift of two little brothers, brothers that momma cherished all of her life.

But there were still many hardships in her childhood. Less than a year later, she nearly died of pinworms and as Pappy's jobs shifted from one area to the next, they continuously moved from house to house. Being the only girl among four boys she was made to carry water and help with the cooking and cleaning, chores that in those days were strictly women's work, while her brothers sat with Pappy learning to pick music and stomp out a tune.

My heart aches for the little girl that was my mother, for all the injustices and hardships of her childhood. I know that even today with all of our programs to care for children and to protect them from starvation and abuse, all that we do to ensure children get the best possible start, I know that children often fall through the cracks and are neglected and mistreated. I always longed for a way to remove the neglect and the feelings of insecurity that Momma gained from those early years. I would have gladly given her that gift if I could have, but it wasn't in my power to give. All I could ever do was love her as much as I possibly could.

# All in a Name

Tess smiled as she listened to Gina "ooh" and "aah" over the clothing, costumes and other props that Bob had brought with him. The younger woman had thrown herself wholeheartedly into the project and at times Tess thought she would have to tie an anchor to her to keep her grounded; her enthusiasm had her floating on air. Together they had gotten the storage room emptied and set up as a small studio. A paneled divider made a dressing area in the back and Bob had hired an electrician who was to come on Monday and finish rewiring the lighting. Bob had also sent over a makeup table from the modeling studio that his mom had discarded and Tess was repainting it while he and Gina unloaded and logged the costumes and other items.

With a squeal of delight, Gina held up a shiny gold costume. "Look, it's a genie costume!" She held it against her body and folded her arms. "May I grant you your wish, Master?"

Tess couldn't help herself, she burst out laughing. "Okay, now I know where you get your energy, you're a genie aren't you? Gina the genie." She teased.

Gina giggled. "You know my dad wanted to name me Jeannie, with a J, after that old show, *I Dream of Jeannie*, but my mom wouldn't let him. They finally settled on Regina, but he's always called me Ginny."

"Maybe we can use that in our advertising somehow." Bob teased. "Maybe we'll put you in the costume and add a tagline like, 'Our Genie can grant your wish for beautiful photographs!'"

Gina frowned and stuck her tongue out at him. "Bleech, I don't think so!" The three of them had become very relaxed together in a short space of time while putting in a lot of hours working closely on a project they were all excited about. Gina and Bob seemed to derive pleasure out of turning everything into a competition or simply in picking on each other, usually to Tess's amusement.

Shaking her head with a grin at their antics, Tess turned back to her painting. It was certainly never a dull moment listening to their banter, and it seemed Bob enjoyed trying to make her laugh as often as possible. She couldn't remember the last time she'd had this much fun in a professional capacity. It was exciting to be so actively involved in a new endeavor, to be challenged and creative and to work with others who were as enthused as she was only added to the pleasure.

"So let's see, Gina was named for a genie; I was named after my grandmother Roberta. Where'd your name come from Tess?" Bob asked.

She shook her head. "Oh no, I don't have to answer that question. I'm not a part of whatever competition the two of you have going on!" Keeping her back to them, she continued her painting.

"Excuse me, girl, but I think you are! You're the one who called me a genie! I think that started this whole conversation!" Gina retorted.

Tess couldn't help her snort of laughter at the stern tone of Gina's voice. "I can't tell you, you'd just laugh."

Bob solemnly drew a large X over the center of his chest. "I won't laugh, cross my heart," bringing howls of laughter from both women. "What? What's so funny?" He tried to be serious but couldn't keep the smile from his face. "Come on Tess, it can't be that bad. Tess is a beautiful name."

His eyes seemed so sincere when he looked at her that she could feel her face grow warm. Chastising herself she quickly turned away. After all, he hadn't said she was beautiful. She carefully balanced the paint brush on the edge of the table and wiped her hands on the cloth dangling from the back pocket of her jeans. She stood tall and stretched her back, smiling as she shook her head. "Okay, here goes, I was named for the cowboy song, 'Mariah.'"

"Mariah," Bob spoke the word softly, "I remember that song." Clearing his throat he sang a familiar line, slightly off key, He grinned. "Is that the right song?"

"Yup, that's it. My brother was really into cowboys, so he went around singing that song all the time. My mom liked it and chose my name from it."

Bob snapped his fingers. "From *Paint Your Wagon*, right?" At Tess's nod he continued. "Okay, but which are you, wind or rain or fire?"

Tess giggled. "That I can never remember; it's either fire or rain because..."

"The wind is called Mariah," they said in unison.

Tess continued to giggle, but as Bob studied her face she grew uncomfortable, especially when his gaze drifted downward and seemed to linger on the curve of her breasts, beneath the old faded sweatshirt she wore. "I think you're probably fire," he said at last, something in his tone making her quickly pull her gaze away from his.

"What do you think, Gina? Am I fire?"

Gina shook her head with a grin. "Girl, you're fire and rain, and hell, you're the wind too when you get to working real hard. You blow up a storm all by yourself."

They all laughed and Tess felt herself relax again. She still felt uncomfortable around Bob alone and was always grateful for the younger woman's presence. Leaning back against the unpainted edge of the makeup table, she watched her two companions as they worked. They were sorting items by theme and carefully numbering and tagging each costume. The number was then logged onto a spreadsheet with a brief description before the costume was covered and hung numerically on the large rack that filled one entire wall of the room. The numbering system would make it easier to locate and control each costume and prop when things got busy. It would also help in identifying items used in a particular setting or for pulling and organizing the desired costumes in advance.

When Bob turned to find her watching them, he flashed his million watt smile, the one that was beginning to have an effect on her, the one that made her knees feel wobbly and her stomach dance. "I think you're right, Gina, Tess is both fire and rain. Some days, she won't smile at all and you look up expecting to see a cloud hanging above her head. But other days, she's like the sunshine and just looking at her you almost need your sunglasses." His words were spoken sincerely, with no hint of teasing and Tess could only continue to stare at him, unable to form a response.

Gina looked at her boss, sensing the other woman's confusion. "Be nice, Bob. Tess has three kids at home; she can't help her mood swings. Three kids are enough to keep anybody confused!" She didn't want Bob to hurt Tess's feelings. Tess was the best boss she'd ever had and she was giving her a chance to do something new and exciting. She didn't want him to upset her in any way.

"Oh, I am being nice. I don't mind her moods, and I like the rain."

The soft sincerity of his voice caused Gina to look at him sharply. *So that's how it is*, she thought, *the man has a soft spot for Tess!* She glanced at her boss; of course poor Tess was too shy to notice. She'd often wondered why she never dated. She'd watched her around men, and if a guy showed the slightest hint of interest, she immediately turned cold and dismissive until he gave up. Bobby had told her the stories about Tess and the married guy, but then Bobby loved to gossip. He'd also told her what he knew of Tess's ex—with his drinking problems—so she figured Tess had plenty of good cause not to trust men. But Bob, he was different; he seemed like one of the good guys, and he'd be a catch. He was good looking; hell, he was dreamy good looking, even if he was too old for her tastes—he was still hot. He was educated, a gentleman with class and manners. He was just what Tess needed. A sly smile crept across her face as she looked from one to the other. Maybe it was time to do a little matchmaking, and maybe, if the interest she felt from Bob was genuine, she wouldn't even have to.

Still under twenty-five, Gina hadn't given up on love yet and she wanted everyone to be happy. In her estimation, happiness came from being in love. Gina fell in and out of love frequently, but she knew one day she'd get it right. She chuckled to herself; this project was turning out to be even more fun than she'd thought!

"So where'd Tressa's name come from?" she asked, wanting to ease the tension she saw on the other woman's face before her 'flight' response kicked in and sent her running from the room on some pretense.

"Um..." Tess looked at the floor, nibbling at her lower lip before responding, "That was kind of an accident."

"You named your daughter by accident?" Gina's voice was filled with incredibility. "How'd that happen?"

Tess smiled. "Yeah, it was sort of an accident. I had always wanted to name a daughter Teresa and call her Terrie. I have a childhood friend; her name is Teresa. I call her my twin because both our names start with T and we were born only a few days apart, in the same hospital. Both of our fathers had died when we were the same age, and ironically we ended up living next door to each other. I thought Teresa was a cool name, much cooler than Tess. And then I found out that Terrie was a nickname for Teresa and that was totally cool, so that's what I wanted to name my daughter. But Billy wasn't sold on the idea. He wanted our daughter to have a proper name, not a nickname. His name is just Billy, not William, or Bill and he didn't want that for our child so Terrie was out. And if we named her Teresa, he wanted it spelled with T-H; he thought it looked better that way." Tess paused, looking back it seemed ridiculous, but it was the truth, they had argued over the spelling of the name. "Eventually, we agreed on the shorter spelling. T-E-R-E-S-A."

When she paused again, Bob asked, "So how'd you end up with Tressa?" He watched the play of emotions on her face and sensed that something was painful in the story and the telling brought up unhappy memories.

She sighed, "Well, when the hospital came for the information for the birth certificate, I was feeding the baby. So Billy filled out the forms." A small melancholic smile crossed her face as she continued. "I guess he'd been celebrating her birth a little too much and he misspelled her name. He wrote T-R-E-S-A." She shook her head. "Later, because of the unusual spelling they came back to me and asked if it was correct. I thought about it and decided that I liked Tressa; it made an even cooler name than Terrie and was still close enough to my friend Teresa's name to make me happy. So I added an extra S and made it Tressa!" Something in the tone of her voice, a hint of defiance mingled with hurt, had changed the atmosphere in the room and things were quieter as they turned back to their work.

*A drinking man*, Bob thought as he helped Gina cover and hang a flamboyant sequined gown with a feather boa attached, momentarily reflecting that he couldn't imagine any woman wanting her pictures made in that costume but his mom had insisted he take it. Glancing over his shoulder, his thought turned back to their conversation. Tess had just revealed that her ex was a drinker, which explained why she had hesitated at lunch when the three of them had gone to celebrate the new venture. He had ordered white wine to drink a toast and she'd seemed reluctant to join in; she hadn't refused but had barely sipped from the slender fluted glass while she ate.

Pausing in his work, his eyes were drawn to her narrow shoulders as she carefully spread paint along the curved legs of the old oak makeup table, covering the many layers of previous paint jobs it had endured over the years. Like the table, Tess was hidden in layers, carefully applied over the years to hide the pain and disappointment she had faced. He longed to unwrap the layers, to find the beauty of the true Tess, to see her happy and fulfilled.

Shocked at where his thoughts were heading, he gave himself a mental shake. *Whoa Bob! Sure, she's attractive, but this woman is a mother; she isn't someone to have a casual fling and besides, she has made it clear that she's not interested in romance or anything else you've got going through your mind. So back off and cool the fantasies before you hurt her even more.* But he couldn't resist one last glance, she seemed so all alone, Tess against the world.

Maybe he could just be a friend, one who would be there for her and not let her down. But then how did he know that; he didn't know what her expectations were. Hell, she hardly seemed to expect anything from anyone. Her attitude seemed to be if she couldn't do it herself, it just wouldn't get done. He could almost hear her say to herself, 'If you don't ask for much, then you won't be disappointed when you don't get it." *Had anyone ever really cared about this woman in her entire life? Had any man ever made her feel loved and cherished? Had there ever been anyone she could truly lean on?* The thoughts continued to turn in his mind as he watched her.

"Bob?" Gina's voice startled him and he realized he'd let his thoughts carry him off again. Making an effort to put Tess from his mind, he turned back to the large trunk of clothing and continued with his work.

# BABY

November 15

Memories flicker and dance inside my head like shiny prisms of glass with the sun's rays reflecting on their surfaces. They sparkle and shimmer, just out of reach, so that I get only fragments, like the taste of some long ago dessert that still lingers on the tongue, or the fragrance of someone's perfume that lies in the stillness of the air long after they are gone. Just a glimpse, a swift picture that must be played in slow motion, over and over again to bring back all of the images, to make the picture clear. Some are so fragmented that I wonder if they are memories at all or only images from long forgotten dreams lingering there in my mind.

The thing about memories is that they are uniquely ours, seen only from our perspective; and we have the power to make them either better or worse than they actually were. We can try and see them through the eyes of others or we can hang onto our anger, our fear or joy, and see only with our own eyes, our own perspective, as we choose. Like writing, producing, and directing our own movie, we can replay it as many times as we like to a captive audience of one, allowing them to live indefinitely inside our psyche, bringing either pain or joy each time they are replayed, flittering inside our heads like butterflies caught in a net. But if we choose, we can release them and allow them to live briefly in the sun before they drift away. Once they are shared with the world even if they return, it is never with the same intensity because suddenly we realize we have survived, and all that holding onto all of those old memories has done is hold us back, kept us trapped in a past that should be over and done.

When I think of the change in emotions memories can evoke as they filter through one's mind, I realize that it is much like the patterns formed on a graph during an electroencephalogram. The peaks and valleys, the highs and lows, the sudden spikes so accurately duplicate our joys and sorrows, our sudden surprises. While all EEG patterns match to a certain degree, as life imitates life, each is also truly unique; just as memories are uniquely ours, our pain, and our joy; special because they are our own.

I know that it is possible to share at least part of these thoughts and feelings with another human being; to have someone so in tune with our thoughts that they understand how we feel without words; or when words are needed, to have someone who truly listens to what we have to say. I know that much of my loneliness comes from having no one to share the joys, triumphs, even the sorrows of my life. It creates an odd ache inside of me, a memory of being *connected* to another that I have never actually experienced, as if my soul remembers and knows that this exists, as if it cries out for this sharing. I realize that part of the distancing that I feel between me and others is of my own making. Whenever anyone gets too close, too personal, my defenses rise automatically, like the sharp barbs of a porcupine's quills, and I push them away.

Looking back on my years with Billy, I realized that I called his indifference closeness. All those times he remained silent—while I talked and made plans—I took for agreement, when in reality he was quiet because it took too much effort to disagree with me or to make plans of his own. He let me think that he agreed and then when he let me down or disappointed me, I was hurt, never seeing that I shared the blame for my disappointment. I had chosen to try and transform a passive and dependent type of personality into a take charge, more involved kind of person, and in my stubbornness, refused to believe at first that it was never going to happen. This effort in futility taught me two important lessons. I now realize that you can't change anyone else; you can't push someone else to do anything at all, no matter how strong your will is. Self-change and the willingness to put forth the effort to change must come from within. The second lesson was a little less obvious, but I now realize that if we want to be involved with a *doer*, one who will help us achieve things, either in our personal lives or in business, then you can't choose someone who always readily agrees with your plans. You have to choose someone who has ideas and input of their own; someone who may question your decisions and choices. Because two minds working together in harmony towards a common goal can push each other onto greater discoveries than one mind working alone.

It has been great working with Ross; he always encourages me to share my opinions, my thoughts and ideas, even if they differ from his own. And I love watching him experience this same type of sharing on an even deeper level with Becky. They seem so in tune with one another, frequently finishing each other's sentences, without the malice you often see in couples who have been together for too long instead, with complete understanding of the other's thoughts. So while I doubt the existence of such a person for myself, I know that some have found it.

I think so few find this type of connection because most people just *settle* on someone. I think many women still look for a meal ticket, and men think if the sex is good they'll be happy. But effort must come from both sides to build true closeness. It takes effort to be willing to listen even when we're tired; to put another's needs, if not ahead of, then at least equal to, our own. Effort to tolerate grumpy moods and down days; effort to remember that the person we love is still there inside even when they're angry on the outside. This effort, this conscious choice to put someone else so prominently in our thoughts whenever we make any type of decision in our lives is what builds the closeness, the connection that truly binds two people together.

Of course, you have to reach the first level of closeness before you can progress, and after living with Billy and then the fiasco with Troy, the idea of even starting a relationship, of even attempting to reach that first level, terrifies me. I feel desire, I long to share my life with someone, but I am too scared. It's better this way; no peaks, no valleys, just flat plains. At least I know what to expect each morning and the idea of more failure is terrifying. It's deeper than my failed marriage. In fact it goes much farther back than that and I don't know if I could ever recover from another betrayal. But then again maybe I have never really recovered at all.

The little white farmhouse snuggled gently into the curve of the mountainside. A bubbly stream flowed behind while a winding dirt road curved above. The spring air laid still and soft over it all; a slight hint of moisture gliding upward as the early morning sun's rays peaked over the mountaintop. In the chicken coop, which sat about twenty yards from the house, a rooster slowly stretched his wings and waddled out into the barnyard. He scratched the dirt and flapped his wings, emitting a few strangled practice crows before flying to a fence post to do the honors of announcing a new day.

The occupants of the little house were already up and about, smoke rose softly from the chimney and light shone from a window. Suddenly, the front door banged open and then shut as a boy, already grown to man height but still awkward with his size, stepped out into the chill morning air. He moved to the gate by the chicken coop and let himself into the pasture beyond, the pigs grunted a greeting as he passed, their pink noses snuffling the air as they waited for their breakfast.

The boy moved quickly, familiar with the routine as he went about his chores, glancing back at his home as he worked. His uncle, only a few years older, worked at the chop block by the house. The soft kerchunk of his ax floated on the still morning air as he chopped wood for Momma's woodstove; she still preferred cooking with wood to using the new bottled gas range Daddy had bought her. Together, they would feed and water the farm animals and carry a supply of wood to the wood box before heading to school.

Pausing in his work, he watched the smoke curling up from the chimney and his stomach rumbled knowing that Momma was preparing breakfast. Fried eggs, bacon, sausage, and big, soft homemade biscuits smothered in home churned butter, along with a piping hot pan of milk gravy. Momma would probably set out a jar of her homemade blackberry jam and maybe even some apple butter, along with lots of fresh cow's milk to wash it all down. The kids at school might tease him and call him "farm boy" because his clothes weren't as new as theirs, and he usually wore work boots to school, but he didn't mind. His clothes were always clean and neat, and if being a farm boy meant having plenty to eat when he knew many children in the area didn't, then he'd be a farm boy any day.

He was proud of their farm, of the crops they grew and preserved; proud of the little white farmhouse his daddy had built himself. But it was a false pride, a pride to cover ugly wounds, ugly truths that they all worked hard to hide. Truths that they all pretended didn't exist. The ugly truth was that just a short ways up the small creek, under the darkness of woods, sat his daddy's moonshine still. Hidden in the crook of a gnarled old oak's roots, buried under last fall's leaves, it sat waiting 'til next time. Strong, sturdy barrels wrapped with shiny copper bands. Under the cover of darkness, he and his uncle had hidden many sacks of half gallon jars of moonshine in the hillsides around their home. Though only a boy of twelve, he could, at this very moment, think of where three jars still lay hidden in the woods in back of the house.

Hell, his daddy wasn't the only one in these hills that made and sold moonshine. When the mines were slow, like now, most everyone did something to earn a dollar; not all of it legal though. The shine paid for their school clothes and bought their gifts at Christmas. No, the shame didn't come from making the shine or from selling it, the shame came from the fact that his daddy drank it himself, and not just a taste now and then. The truth was that—his daddy was a drunk. Not that he would ever say those words out loud, Momma would smack his mouth if he did, but they were the truth all the same. Daddy didn't drink every day and sometimes he didn't drink for months. But in the past few years especially since baby's birth, it had been harder and harder for him to stop and sober up once he started.

This last time had been one of the worst. Daddy hadn't worked now for two weeks and even though Momma had called his boss and told him he was sick, they all knew she was worried that his boss wouldn't hold his job much longer. Without a paycheck, how long could they survive? He shifted his gaze to the upper pastures above the road. The money crops were there and he knew the crops would be all right; he and Grant would see to that. With the garden coming in soon, he knew they would have food, but cash money had to go for some things, like the electric bill, the phone bill, and gas for the cook stove.

Suddenly, he knew why Momma pretended to prefer the cantankerous old wood stove to the shiny new gas range. It was because wood was free. She never said much but he'd noticed the lines of worry in her face. The last time Daddy had started drinking he'd stayed drunk for two months and he knew she was worried he would do that again. If they could just survive the summer, he knew that Grant would see that the corn and potato crops were sold and money would come in to pay the bills.

If only he were a grown man, he would work hard and bring Momma the money he earned. He smiled to himself, feeling the pride he would have if he could give her money to pay the bills and maybe even some extra to buy her something pretty. Uncle Grant teased him and called him "momma's boy," and maybe he was, but that was okay, Momma needed someone to take care of her.

Baby lay silently in the big double bed she shared with her sister. It was an iron stead bed with coil springs beneath the mattress and she knew if she touched the bedstead it would be cool to her touch. Her blue eyes watched the dust particles that hung suspended in the bright shaft of sunlight that streamed through the window. She could hear the muted voices of Momma and Becca as they prepared breakfast, but she felt far removed from them. Her small hands idly plucked at the soft cotton ties of her mother's quilt, her tiny brow furrowed in thought.

She was still called Baby even though she'd just passed her fourth birthday. She knew her letters and her numbers and could count to one hundred, forwards and backwards, and she didn't yet mind being called Baby; it made her feel special. As if she were the hub around which her family turned, important to each of them but in different ways. She knew how to please them, to befriend them in the way that suited best. Artful in her role as the youngest, she could be alternately small and in need of help, or wiser than her years when a sympathetic ear was needed. She could fade silently into the moment or be cheerful and talkative; tease and wrestle with her brother or cuddly and quiet with her sister, whatever was needed. It never occurred to her to use her skills to manipulate them to get her own way though she often unknowingly did just that. She just liked being there for each of them.

Most of the time, her charm worked on Daddy as well, but lately there had been too many days like yesterday, days when he hardly seemed to know she was there at all. It frightened her to not be able to get his attention, to be told to go away and not bother him, to quietly watch as he lay on the couch in the living room and drank beer after beer, or hot toddies made with homemade moonshine. She could sometimes see his hands tremble as he held the cup to his mouth and it frightened her. This was her daddy—her big strong daddy, who swung her up into the air and gave her bear hugs when he came home from work. Of course lately, he hadn't been going to work; he'd been home all day with her and Momma while everyone else was at school, but all he did was lay there on the couch. He didn't play with her or let her tag along while he worked around the farm.

Her eyes suddenly grew tense as she replayed the scene from the night before in her mind. It had been the dead of night when the last trace of light from the day had passed and dawn was still hours away. She had awakened to the sound of someone banging on the bedroom door. Her father's drunken voice had called through the door, demanding that Uncle Grant get up to drive him to buy beer. Legally, Uncle Grant was barely old enough to drive and he still didn't have his license, but he'd actually already been driving for several years whenever Daddy was drunk. Momma always said, "Better Grant gets a ticket than your dad wrecks and kills someone."

Frightened, she had sat up in bed and started to cry out, but Grant's whisper from the other big bed across the room where he and Wesley slept had warned them all to stay quiet. Becca had held her and she had snuggled against the warmth, her eyes wide with fear in the darkness. Daddy had continued banging on the door, rattling the knob and yelling; his voice loud and hoarse in the quietness of the night. But Momma had wisely locked the door when she said good night; she must have known he was almost out of beer. Then Momma's soft voice had reached them as she quietly pleaded with Daddy to go back to bed. After much loud arguing on his part, he had finally given in and they had settled nervously back beneath the covers. Baby had soon fallen into a restless sleep and now she felt tired and grumpy.

She wondered now if it had all just been a dream, but then Becca came to get her up for breakfast and as she looked at her sister's tired face, she knew it had been real. Feeling frightened by the look of fear and defeat on her sister's face, she demanded that she go away. "Not you, go away, I want my momma. Momma... MOMMIE!" She yelled as she scooted to the back of the bed. Crying louder as Rebecca reached for her, she angrily pushed her away. "No, I want my momma!" She didn't feel like smiling and being a sweet little girl. After all, how could Becca comfort her when she looked so upset herself? She needed a higher authority to assure her that all was right in the world. She needed a parent. "Mommmmieeeeee!"

Stunned, Becca backed away from the bed wondering what was wrong with Baby as she never behaved this way. She watched as her mother dried her hands on her apron and angrily marched to the bedroom. Seeing the lines of worry on her mother's face, she knew that she had no patience for Baby's tantrum. She should have handled it herself. Turning back, she quietly held her arms out and motioned for Baby to come to her.

But Baby saw her mother and smiled her happiness before noticing the worry in her face. "Cut out the nonsense, Baby, and get out of that bed. Now!" her mother demanded.

One look at her momma's hands planted with determination on her hips and Baby quickly did as she was told. Momma wasn't going to offer any comfort. Leaping from the bed, she ran to Becca who scooped her up and carried her to the table. The boys were washing up from their chores and Wes stuck his tongue out at her as they passed the sink. She promptly returned the favor as Becca settled her into her old fashioned wooden high chair that she still used when they sat around the table. Wes's gesture made her feel a little better, that somehow things were still normal here.

The boys quietly sat down at the table and no one spoke as they filled their plates. Baby looked around the table and wondered where her daddy was and why he wasn't joining them for breakfast? She leaned to look towards his and Momma's bedroom but the door was closed. Confused, she finally asked only to be told he didn't feel well so he was still in bed. Baby silently digested this bit of information; which must mean he would be home on the couch again today.

"It's called a hangover," Grant suddenly said as he shoveled biscuits smothered in gravy into his mouth.

"Grant! Don't be telling them that," Momma scolded.

"Why not? It's the truth."

Momma looked around the table at each of them, "Don't any of y'all repeat that, you hear me?" She angrily looked at Grant. "You ought to be ashamed of yourself talking about your brother that way. He provides us all with plenty to eat and we have a warm home so don't you be talking bad about him, especially in front of the others."

Grant put his fork down and looked at his plate for a moment. "He works us all like dogs to provide this food, while he lays there and pours another drink down his throat…" Shaking his head, he rose and left the table without another word. They could hear the front door as it banged shut behind him.

No one spoke and the tension in the room mounted like the air before a storm when it grew heavy with expectation. A vice seemed to tighten somewhere deep inside of Baby's stomach. What if he left and never came back? What would they do without him? He was a part of her family and her family seemed to be falling apart. She worked hard to hold them all together but she couldn't seem to do that anymore. She couldn't seem to make them smile or laugh anymore. They always seemed tense and snappy with each other and impatient with her. She must have done something very, very bad. Staring at the floral pattern on her plate, Baby's vision blurred as the vice in her stomach tightened. Suddenly, the food in her stomach boiled over and she leaned forward and threw up in her plate.

# Madness

November 23

There have been times in my life when I have seen the doorway to madness. It has beckoned me with its promise of sweet relief from the pain and depression of living and I have thought of surrendering to its release. To soar amidst the world of blankness, to serenely forget one's problems, to be cared for, fed and given a bed where one's only cares are of the demons inside. But those demons are large and dark and never ending, and no one can remove them but self, so to enter that door would be like falling into a void of blackness with no end, a bottomless pit of nameless terrors where the only limit would be the creativity of one's own imagination. The climb back out would be long, hard and torturous, each step a bullet of pain as the demons strive to hold their captive. Better to never enter that world at all than to suffer the struggles of trying to escape. For some, however, the fall is sudden, without warning. They never see the doorway, only the free fall after they have passed through, and then it is too late, much too late.

*My father spent time in drug rehab centers for his drinking in the last years of his life, where in those days, the insane were also kept. I remember visiting him one Sunday on a warm autumn day. We sat in the courtyard of the old hospital, high on a hill, overlooking a picturesque small town built along the curving banks of a meandering river in one of Virginia's many beautiful valleys. To look down on that view, you would never imagine a more peaceful setting could be found. The sky was a bright blue above, with soft, lazy clouds floating high in the atmosphere, and the hillsides resounded with colors from God's palette as the trees, dressed in all their autumn glory, softly swayed in the gentle breeze that fanned the hilltops. Squirrels chattered nearby, unafraid of the humans who gathered at the stone benches placed along the sidewalks that wound beneath several old oak trees. They happily gathered the fallen acorns and quickly grabbed any handouts that were tossed their way as well; their bushy tails swishing to and fro as they worked.*

*It was like a visit to a peaceful park, until you turned around and witnessed the madness, the stark terror on the faces of some of the patients at the barred upper windows of the sedate old building, which had been built to look like an eighteenth century plantation house. The strangeness of it all fascinated as well as frightened me, and I gazed back at those faces until my mother reminded me that it was impolite to stare. Still, I couldn't resist an occasional peak at the poor tortured souls who clung to the bars, not as if they longed to get out, but as if they feared the world getting in.*

*Sitting on a bench, my bare legs rocking against its coldness, I munched on the peanut butter crackers my mother had brought for me and watched the trees' reflection in the shiny toes of my black patent leather shoes. My father's hands shook as he puffed at his cigarette, desperately trying to light it, and I watched as Uncle Grant cupped his brother's hands in his own and held them steady until the flame ignited the tobacco. My father took a long inhalation, sighing contentedly; he could only smoke on weekend visits and it had been a long hard week for him, deprived of both cigarettes and alcohol. The two of them joined my mother where she stood by the stone fence that edged the courtyard, leaving me sitting alone on the bench.*

*I tipped my head back to watch as two frisky squirrels chased each other up a tree. Breaking my cracker in half, I tossed the pieces out to them and watched as they each raced to retrieve their respective halves, each chattering a warning scold to the other as they ran back to the tree. When I again looked up, I realized that someone had sat down on the bench next to me. Frightened, I scooted forward, carefully pulling my dress from underneath me as I moved to keep from tearing it on the rough, concrete surface of the bench.*

*Glancing sideways at my companion, I saw that it was a woman, though she wore rough men's brogans with a dark brown coat that reached nearly to her ankles. Her head was covered in a scarf that was the same tan color as my button up sweater, and she held tightly to a shiny brown vinyl purse. Just as I prepared to jump down from the bench, she suddenly held a Little Debbie cake out to me. She didn't say a word, just pushed the snack cake towards my hands. I saw that it was an oatmeal cake like the ones Momma sometimes packed in Daddy's lunch.*

*Uncertain of what to do, for I had been carefully warned by my siblings not to talk to any of the nuts here at the nuthouse, I looked directly at her face for the first time. She had carefully applied a bright shiny coat of red lipstick, a full half inch above her upper lip, creating the appearance of a bright red mustache. The image was so startling, the bright red such a contrast to her otherwise drabness, that I smiled. She smiled back and again pressed the cake into my hands. I looked from her face to her hands, wanting to accept the treat, sensing that it would please her if I did. I noticed that her hands were rough and dry but the nails had been painted a bright red to match her lipstick though the polish over ran the actual nail and covered most of the tips of her fingers as well.*

*"Take it Tess, and tell her thank you." My father's voice startled me and I jumped in response. "Take the cake," he repeated when I made no move to do so.*

*Hearing the edge to his voice, I quickly snatched the cake from her hand and mumbled a thank-you. She reached out and gently patted the top of my head. "Pretty girl," she croaked her voice dry and crackly like the autumn leaves under foot when I walked on them, and I recognized the sound as the sound of a voice that hadn't been used in awhile. "Very pretty little girl," she said again, this time slowly tilting her head to look up at my father.*

*"Thank you," he told her, grabbing my arm and yanking me up off the bench so suddenly that the concrete chaffed my legs and I lost my balance and fell against him. He pulled my arm harder, jerking me upright onto my feet and then he led me swiftly along the sidewalk to where my mother and Grant stood by the stone fence. "Don't ever do that again!" he scolded; his voice low but hard as steel. "Never! Do you understand me?" I nodded, not knowing exactly what it was that I was to never do again, but I feared his anger too much to ask.*

*My mother snatched the cake from my hands and dropped it into a trash can, holding it by the edge as if it were poisoned, and then brushed my clothes from head to toe as if I had somehow risked contamination of madness by sitting next to the old woman. Embarrassed, I looked down at my shoes, their shiny finish now a mockery of how I felt inside. I deliberately scuffed the toes against the stone work which brought me a whack to my rear from my mother. "Stop that and behave or we won't let you come again," she scolded.*

*"Good," I mumbled while fighting back my tears. Head still bowed, I stole a glance over at the bench where the old woman still sat. She looked so sad sitting there all alone with her bright red clown lips and her big shiny purse; she sure didn't look harmful, just sad. She stared back at me for a long time, softly mouthing the words "pretty, pretty little girl" to herself. Then opening her big handbag, she took out a baby doll and cuddled it in her arms. Stroking the molded hair, she hummed a lullaby that I could softly hear as the wind gently blew the sounds to me, drying my tears as it whispered through my hair, lifting the strands from my collar. I watched as she kissed the doll's head, leaving lipstick stains behind, and then closed her eyes, seeming to sleep there*

with the autumn sunshine filtering down through the trees. Even then, I could feel her sadness like a burden on my soul, and I longed to defy my parents and return to sit beside her, to offer comfort somehow.

Sensing my confusion, Uncle Grant took my hand in his. "I think we'll take a walk, leave you two alone for awhile," he told my parents as he led me away.

We walked in silence. Grant has never been one for words, but his quiet understanding soothed me and soon I felt brave enough to ask, "Grant, why'd Momma throw the cake away?"

"Because you shouldn't take food from strangers," he replied. We had stopped by a row of hedges, facing away from the courtyard towards the parking lot. I could see our old, blue Buick, the sunlight glinting off the windshield and suddenly, I longed to be safe inside, heading for home.

"Why'd he make me take it then? Daddy, I mean. Why'd he make me?" I asked.

"Cause your momma didn't want to hurt the old lady's feelings."

I thought about this as I watched a white coated attendant climb out of a green Chevy and head for the steps leading up to where we stood. "Someone already hurt her feelings real bad. I don't think it matters no more."

"Anymore," Grant automatically corrected my grammar, "and I think you're right Baby. I think someone already hurt her real bad."

I ran my hands over the prickly leaves of the hedges where they had been trimmed nice and neat. Not like the woods at home where the bushes could grow free, these had to behave, fit a mold, a pattern. Sort of like the world intruding on the old lady. Maybe she didn't behave like everyone else, or wear her makeup like everyone else, but did it matter? She wasn't hurting anyone. "I wish I'd never asked Momma to let me come. I don't like this place."

The attendant reached the top of the steps just as I uttered these words and he stopped to smile at me; his hands on his hips in mock surprise. "What's this? You don't like it here? Why not?" He stooped down to eye level, his smile sincere.

*Feeling embarrassed to have been overheard; I bowed my head, nervously plucking at the leaves of the boxwood that grew in the hedgerow. Glancing up, I could see that he waited for an answer so I shrugged my shoulders. "Everyone seems so sad; sad or crazy." I looked up to gauge his reaction to my words. His eyes were brown with little flecks of gold that seemed to radiate the warmth from the sun. I could see sympathy in those eyes and I felt an uncanny urge to wrap my arms around his neck and have him hug me. "Is my daddy crazy too?" I asked softly, looking back down at the crushed leaves in my hand.*

*Recognizing Grant from previous visits, I saw him glance up at him and then over to my parents before he answered, "No, honey, your dad's not crazy; he has a disease. A sickness called alcoholism and we're trying to help him get better." He smoothed a strand of windblown hair from my face as I fought to keep the tears from my eyes. "Do you understand?" he asked.*

*I studied his face and thought; I bet if he had a little girl he would always take care of her. I bet he'd care how she was doing in school and would read her bedtime stories and things like that. He wouldn't drink all the time and have to stay in the nuthouse to get better.*

*"Sweetheart, do you understand?" he asked again. At my nod, he patted the top of my head as he stood. "Good, now I better get to work." With a nod at Grant, he started to move away.*

*"Do you have any little girls?" I shocked myself by blurting out the question, my face warm with embarrassment. What if he knew what I was thinking? What if he knew I wanted him to take me home with him? Where I would be safe and not have to come to the nuthouse to visit my daddy anymore.*

*"No darling, I don't. But I have two little boys. They're older than you though. They like to play basketball. Do you ever play basketball?" I liked the way he talked directly to me and not just at me, as if I were an object instead of a person, the way so many grownups did. There was no patronizing tone in his voice, just genuine concern and interest in the conversation. In that moment I tried to gather courage to ask him if I could go home with him. I had never wanted to go live with*

anyone else before, but this man had such sincere eyes. He made me feel secure just in talking to me. I knew he would never let anything bad happen to me. But before the words could form, I thought of my momma, and Becca and Wesley, and even Uncle Grant, and I knew I couldn't leave them.

"No," I whispered my reply, the pain of my realization making me feel torn between those I loved and the hopes of a security I had never known. "But Wesley does. Wesley plays basketball; he's my big brother." I kept my eyes down, not wanting him to detect the disappointment in mine.

"And what's your name?" he asked.

"Tess," I replied, "and this is my Uncle Grant," I mumbled. Sorry now that I had prolonged our conversation.

"Well, it's nice to meet you, Tess. My name is Larry and I have enjoyed talking to you, but now I really better get to work before my boss gets mad at me." When I glanced up at him, I saw that he was smiling warmly down at me. "I'll look for you on the next visitation day and don't worry about your daddy, he'll be just fine. And I promise he's not crazy."

Grant took my hand as I turned to watch Larry hurry towards a side entrance to the hospital, his white lab coat billowing behind him. Again, I briefly fantasized that he could take me with him and that he could be my new daddy, but I knew it was just make-believe. As the big double doors closed tightly behind him with a soft swoosh and the clatter of a locking mechanism, I thought, You're wrong buddy, my daddy is crazy. He's just a crazy drunk.

# CHOICES AND DECISIONS

April 3, 19??

I took the kids to church today for Easter services, and then afterwards we saw a Disney movie and went for ice cream. It was a nice day. But then we came home to find Billy had been out drinking and he was sloppy drunk, saying nasty things to me and trying to grab me inappropriately in front of the kids. It made me hurt inside. I just feel lonely and sad. I wish I could find the words to write the things that are inside of me, trapped there without a way out; I'm not sure that I can, but here goes:

I feel as if I have been swallowed whole, drained, and destroyed. The spark and energy, the hyper, energetic person that was me is all gone. I am a shell, a miserable shell. And I wonder, since they spent the day with just me anyway, wouldn't life be better for my babies if there was just me? If they didn't have to come home after a nice Easter Sunday out and watch me argue with and dodge the hands of, their drunken father?

Of course, he tells his family that I'm the reason we can't ever get ahead; that I'm the one who spends all of our money. Well, I guess he's right that I'm to blame; I spend the money on groceries and clothes for the kids, on medical bills and trying to keep the car running. But of course, I'm the child of a drunk—never as good as decent, churchgoing folks—so I never defended myself, never told them the truth. Those old habits of secrecy are so ingrained, and hey, how dare I think I can get above my raising? So inside, I tell myself that of course it's all my fault, it's my denial of what I am that causes all of our problems. I can still hear the whispers, the words that are probably only imagination, but yet they are there: *Little dirty farm girl, her daddy ain't nothing, he makes 'shine; she's just an ignorant hillbilly.*

Please guide me, Father, I am a feather in the wind.

Admitted 2/5/196?
Discharged 2/9/196?

This is a white male who had onset of nausea and vomiting beginning three days ago and it continued to get progressively worse. Patient also has epigastric pain and symptoms similar to peptic ulcer.

Patient was previously operated on for perforated ulcer two years ago. He did very well following the surgery and indigestion had improved. He had spinal fusion surgery 16 months ago and is still wearing a brace. Patient is unable to work.

Patient had some wheezing and rapid heartbeat on admission. Lab work was all within normal limits but peptic ulcer cannot be ruled out.

Patient was given Ringer's Lactate Solution IV and Morphine on admission. Patient was placed on NPO.

After the second day patient was placed on a bland diet. He did well and his condition improved. He was discharged 4 days post-admission with the abdominal pain cleared. His back is still weak and he wears the brace. He was sent home on a sippy regime and is to follow up in the out-patient department.

October 23, 19??

I am sitting here feeling sorry for myself and so depressed, so overwhelmed with hopelessness. Tonight was Cub Scout pack night and where was Daddy? I don't know. Out drinking I guess. He didn't come home after work, but when we got home he was passed out in bed. As I looked around at the other mommies and daddies with their families, I felt anger, shame, and aching disappointment for my children.

I don't mean to be ungrateful for all that I have, but shouldn't daddies participate and be involved too? I feel so confused. I'm not even sure if I'm a good mother anymore or if I should be doing more and complaining less.

But, let me lift myself out of my doldrums and write of the joy I still find in the world in spite of this. We have had the most beautiful autumn. I've never seen the trees look so beautiful, or do I say that every year? Maybe it's because we had such a dry summer, but on just one tree you can see yellow, green, and orange; even tangerine. It's so pretty that I wish I could paint, or even take really spectacular photos to capture a little of the beauty. And I thank you, Lord, for our beautiful world; help me move forward in the right direction, please.

November 5, 19??

Dear Diary, this is the first time I've written to a diary, but I think I'm gonna like it. My sister, Rebecca, bought you for me when we stopped in town after school today.

Freddie, that's my boyfriend. Well, that's who I like. I don't know if he likes me or not. But things went well between us today. We have a lot of classes together and we talk a lot.

When Becca and I started home today after we stopped in town, she could only get the car to go in reverse. It was because she'd left the emergency brake on, but we backed in a complete circle around the entire parking lot before she figured out what was wrong. She was embarrassed but I thought it was so funny.

November 6, 19??

Dear Diary, we went for a ride today and on the way home we picked up Toby, my neighbor Donna's boyfriend. He was hitch-hiking. I can't stand Donna. She thinks she's so gorgeous, but Toby sure is cute!

Roy, my mom's boyfriend, just came to pick her up. They're going to visit a friend who's in the hospital and Becca's out tonight too so I'm home alone.

November 8, 19??

Dear Diary, today didn't go so well. Freddie didn't talk to me very much at all. It's so hard to tell if he likes me or not. James says he likes me again. He used to be my boyfriend. He just got his arm out of the cast and he really did look pretty good today. I just wish I knew for certain if Freddie liked me or not. Oh well.

November 13, 19??

Dear Diary, I just hung around the house all day today. Mom and Roy just got back from dinner and he's asked me a million questions about the movie that's on TV and I'm not even really watching it! Sometimes he really bugs me.

November 15, 19??

Dear Diary, I had a good time at school today. A bunch of us played "Freeze tag" at lunch time, and every time I got caught if anyone said, "Freddie, Tess is frozen," he came and rescued me! We played tag football too and he was helping me a lot then too.

And we didn't have much homework either! Good day.

November 16, 19??

Dear Diary, Freddie wasn't at school today and I missed him.

November 17, 19??

Dear Diary, I can't believe what Becca has done! She told Freddie's older sister, "My little sister likes your little brother." I could have died of embarrassment! How could she do that? Freddie laughed! I wanted to say, "I hate you, Freddie!" But I was too embarrassed to say anything. I'm going to like James now instead.

November 18, 19??

Dear Diary, today wasn't as bad as I expected. Freddie acted like nothing had changed. I hope nothing has. I still can't believe Becca did that!

November 25, 19??

Dear Diary, today is Thanksgiving Day. We had a big dinner with turkey, cranberry sauce, sweet potatoes, mashed potatoes, gravy, and I can't even remember the rest! Rebecca made up a big plate and I took it over to our neighbor, Roma. She's old and doesn't see well. She gave me a big hug and a kiss! It made me feel nice.

November 26, 19??

Dear Diary, me, Becca and Wes went to the donkey basketball game at the high school tonight. Both James and Freddie were there and now I'm even more confused over which one I like best! We had a good time though. At one point, Mr. Butler's donkey (he's my science teacher) laid down right under the basket so he stood up on its back and just plopped the ball through the net! He scored three times that way. It was so funny! Everyone laughed.

November 27, 19??

Dear Diary, nothing much happened today. I just helped Mom clean house, YUCK! Otherwise it was just another drab, dull, boring day. I hate drab days!

November 29, 19??

Dear Diary, I still can't decide who to like best, Freddie or James. James told me today that he loved me and some day he would show me how much! I didn't know what to say because I know I don't love him. Freddie and I get along so well and James sometimes hurts my feelings. If he doesn't like what I'm wearing he'll say, "You don't look good today." Or if he doesn't like what I've done with my hair he'll say, "Don't wear your hair like that, it makes your ears stick out." Things like that hurt and piss me off too! Freddie never says anything mean like that; he never says I look bad. He never tells me I look good either, but at least he doesn't hurt my feelings.

December 25, 19??

Dear Diary, its Christmas Day! I know I haven't written in a long, long time but nothing much has been happening. But today is Christmas! Uncle Grant and Patty came and Wes too. They spent the night and we all sat by the tree last night and listened to Wes play carols on his guitar. We kept all the lights off except the tree lights and it was so beautiful. I got some great stuff too—a new bicycle, a cassette tape recorder, two games, a watch, and some clothes. And everyone helped make Christmas dinner—I mashed the potatoes and baked the rolls—it was very nice!

February 25, 19??

Dear Diary, today was an exceptionally good day! Everyone called me Freddie or Mrs. Freddie and I loved it, although I pretended not to like it! He took a pen from me last week and today he said he was going to give it back to me, so I walked over to his desk, and just as he started to hand it to me, Bill said, "It's about time he gave you an engagement ring." Freddie just laughed and still kept my pen!

February 28, 19??

Dear Diary, today was okay. Some people were still calling me Mrs. Freddie. He still hasn't given my pen back. He says he likes using it 'cause it writes good. Bill says he likes using it 'cause it's mine.

Mrs. Owens, my math teacher, wasn't at school today. Her husband was in a bad mining accident last night; he works evening shift. He was lucky and wasn't hurt too bad so she should be back soon. It reminded me of when Daddy got hurt in the mines when the big rock fell on him. It crushed his back and he had to have spinal surgery and was in a huge cast for a long, long time.

# Patterns and Dreams

March 2, 19??

I have not written to any form of a diary in quite some time, but I find the need returning. I like myself much more than I used to. It's strange. For the first time ever I feel secure with me! I know I'm still too gullible, that I take people too much at face value, and there are times when the old insecurities and the critical self-talk comes back, but mostly, I try to be nice to myself! I have finally realized that Billy's drinking truly has nothing to do with me; I have distanced myself from taking any responsibility for the issues it causes both in our family and in our home.

He comes home drunk and behaves like a childish pest, pinching me, wanting to wrestle with the kids. He gets mad at me because I won't "play" with him, but the truth is, it makes me ill, it makes me so full of rage and anger, and I don't want his drunken attention. I want a partner, not another child.

So, I finally faced up to the fact that I am married to an alcoholic and that doesn't make me a bad person. My entire life I've lived with a drunk or with the stigma of drunkenness. Partially because my life started that way, I felt I deserved no better.

Our entire life revolves around his drinking. School functions and outings are ruined because of it. He embarrasses us and we make excuses for him. It's life with my dad all over again, hide the shame. But I have finally realized, it's not our shame, it's not our fault.

I worry that I could be raising more alcoholics, or a daughter who will feel she deserves no better from a man. I am lonely here, living with him. I am tired of the smell of booze and tired of the disregard he shows for our home; for my feelings. And I wonder, *Would I be any lonelier living as a single parent?* Time will tell I suppose, because I think the time has come.

I know I am depressed right now. I stay tired all of the time; I am sure it's stress. I long for something to focus my energy on, but things just seem so hopeless, so overwhelming. I don't want to just sit and feel sorry for myself, feel sorry for the situation I am in, I want to move forward, to fix things…but there seems to only be one solution.

On a positive note, we had a fluffy white snow late today, and we have a full moon tonight, and looking out at the glistening white on the trees under the silvery moon is so beautiful it almost takes my breath away. And at times like this I feel that "God's in his kingdom, all's right with the world." Well, all may not be right, but God is here and his beauty is all around me and whatever choice I make, I know his love will walk with me and guide me.

VA Hospital Admission: 6-25-196?

44 Year Old Male—Admitted Due to: (Listed in number of importance and mark an X beside of the reason for admission)

(1) Acute brain syndrome, alcohol intoxication(X)
(2) Chronic suppurative Otitis Media, left

Findings summary on discharge:
Second admission of this 44-year-old white, married, unemployed man who has a history of periodic over-indulgence in alcohol for several years. Sprees occur from 6 to 12 months with 2 to 3 weeks of steady drinking. First admission here from 11-17-196? To 11-23-196? because of a seizure induced by alcohol.

Patient worked regularly in the coal mines until he suffered a broken back in a slate fall in April 196?. This was followed by a spinal fusion in July 196? But patient cannot return to his former work and requires a back brace. He and his family subsist on disability payments from the mines and Social Security. Present period of drinking is of 2 months' duration and the patient states he has been drinking, "all I can get a hold of," including beer, wine, and whiskey, but mostly moonshine, up to one-half gallon per day. Eating has been irregular with some vomiting. No trouble with the law. One week ago an attempted withdrawal of alcohol caused him to begin seeing snakes and hearing voices in the room, especially at night. He has been shaky for several days and unable to sleep and entered the hospital at the insistence of his wife.

On admission the patient was approximately oriented for time and place. He appeared tense and shaky. He admits vivid dreams of seeing snakes but denies hallucinations at the moment. Patient expressed a fear of dying from his drinking but was not depressed. No delusionary or paranoid ideation.

Physical examination showed unsteadiness and tremor. The left otic canal showed a purulent drainage with a small perforation of the drum. Blood pressure was 160/110. Upper abdominal midline scar. Surgical scar of lumbar spine area. Neurological examination negative except for tremulousness.

Routine admission laboratory work negative. Transaminase 44, Cephalin Flocculation and Bilirubin normal. X-ray of chest showed no change since last admission. Healing fractures of lower ribs, both sides. Left mastoid showed haziness consistent with chronic infection.

Patient was treated initially with Thorazine and then with Librium 50mgs q.i.d. and Vitamin B. The patient's alcoholic withdrawal subsided quickly. Librium was reduced to 10mgs q.i.d. at discharge. Chronic Otitis Media was treated with Chloromycetin for 7 days. The patient stated that he was going to stop drinking because he felt he would die if he did not. He was discharged 7-23-6?, still unable to do heavy work on account of back injury.

Signed: B Wood, M.D.

November 24

The past is a part of everyone, but for some it is always prominently present within us. It is the wine, the bread and the cheese, the nourishment that creates the foundation of our lives. Much of the focus that gives meaning to our lives is compared to or modeled on things from our past.

The past has always intrigued me, not just my own past but my family's past as well. I pictured my mother as a young girl, so insecure, so in need of love and reassurance; and my Father, who in the beginning was so strong and full of confidence. It's easy to understand why she wanted to marry him, but I don't think my father answered that need in her for very long in spite of her love for him because it wasn't long before his drinking grew to be a constant problem in their lives, and he instead became another burden for her to bear.

He asked a lot of her when he was on a binge; she suddenly had to take charge of everything to do with running our home and the farm, which was a stark contrast to when he was sober as he never included her in financial decisions or allowed her to have control of any of their finances in any way. Then suddenly, for weeks, she was the one left searching for a way to pay the bills, buy groceries, and to run the household. There were times when she reminisced and remembered the good — the strong, self assured young man she fell in love with, but she also clearly remembered the burden he became. She remembered the rages he flew into when he sobered up and realized she had made decisions while he was incapacitated. He was never pleased with the choices she'd made, not because they were bad decisions but simply because she had made them at all, without his permission. To put it bluntly, my Father was a controlling son of a bitch who would beat his children or his spouse into submission if they questioned (or even looked like they were questioning) anything he said.

The only true love my mother ever had as an adult was from her children. But then I guess I could say the same for my own life as well. It's hard not to follow patterns created from birth. Instincts so strong we don't even know they are there until years have passed and we see we have walked the same path as others before us, that we too have looked for love from someone who cannot love us in return, that we have merely added another weave to the fabric of our lives, repeated in the same pattern of those that came before. I need to find a way to stop the pattern and to make my children see the pitfalls. Is that possible? I'm not sure.

I had an epiphany today. For as long as I can remember I have had an irrational fear of snakes. I can barely tolerate toy snakes, and only then if they're not touching me. Even snakes on TV can make me jump in fear, and I quickly change the channel. I have had nightmares about snakes and creepy, crawly things for as long as I can remember as well. Nightmares involving worms and snakes, and worms that turn into snakes, and snakes that hissed and entwined themselves around my body; single snakes that suddenly multiplied into hundreds, crawling all over my body! In my fear, I try and try to scream, but I am so frightened I can't, and when I finally awake, I am sweating and trembling with fear. The dreams have gotten less frequent as an adult, but all through my childhood and teen years I had them often, frequently; waking and crying in my sleep.

Then today, I was remembering when my father slept on a hospital bed in our living room for many months following his spinal surgery. He slept there for over a year while his body slowly healed, and I remember him being drunk in that bed for most of that time. I also remember, at one point in late spring, he tried to sober up so he could attend Becca's graduation. He got DTs and he would scream and cry out that snakes were crawling on his body and that his skin itched, and he would wake swatting, slapping, and clawing his own flesh…and then, like an epiphany, I realized where my nightmares and irrational fears come from. I was a young, impressionable child and I heard his screams and his insistence that there were snakes crawling all over him even though my mom repeatedly told him there was nothing there. These words echoed with a child whose imagination was so vivid, and I incorporated them into my own psyche…it was like a sigh of relief, to finally find a reason for these dreams and these fears that I have battled for as long as I can remember. I doubt my own fears will just disappear now, but at least I have an understanding of how it all started.

It's ironic that I loved my father so much as a child, but I was always a daddy's girl, and yet I can look back and see all the pain and shame and deprivation that he brought to us. All of his life, he was a hard worker except for when he was drinking. He was so well liked, respected even in the community. His family name was well known, after all, there were so many of them since out of his eleven siblings, only two were girls. We could have prospered and been one of the "better families" in our small town but his drinking held us down, kept us in debt. It also stopped us from forming close bonds with anyone so that on the rare occasions that I go back now, I hardly know anyone other than family.

Of course, I still keep in touch with Teresa and Shane, my best friends from childhood, but neither of them live back there anymore either. (Teresa was my "at home" friend, and Shane was my school friend, since Teresa and I went to different schools). Shane and I met just after my thirteenth birthday; she was new in school. Her dad had grown up in the county but then served twenty years in the army, moving from base to base so Shane's only connection to our rural area had been infrequent, brief visits to her grandparents, so she hated it there at first.

The other kids made fun of her accent that stood out among our southern twangs, and I could understand why. Having briefly lived in Detroit before my dad's death, I could remember the Northern children making fun of my Southern drawl. I have since learned to modify my speech, so people hear only a slight Southern tone and usually have difficulty deciding what area of the country I'm from. Knowing just how Shane felt, I defended her against the barbs, empathy having always been my strength as well as my weakness. It is entirely possible to feel another's pain too strongly.

Our friendship grew and I was thrilled to have two best friends, one who needed me and my strength at school, and one who shared the turmoil of being the child of a single mother with me at home. Both listened to my childish philosophies including my already somewhat dismal, negative outlook on life, grown from the disappointments I had already faced.

I had this innate need to share everything about me with them and I wanted to know everything about them in return. We shared "feelings" notes in which we wrote only about the mood we were in for the day and why. I even shared my diary and encouraged them to keep one as well, so we could share that too. For a short time I created a "favorites' collection" and I drew up cards with blanks for comments on little pink index cards that we each had to fill out once a month listing our likes and dislikes: our favorite colors and songs, which guys we had a crush on, and which we just found annoying. After reading these aloud to each other, I then filed them away in a little pink file box and occasionally, we would review the entire collection just to see how our tastes had changed over the months. Generally, which ever friend I was with, Teresa or Shane, it was just the two of us. We didn't hang out with a gang or a group of people. Even then I wasn't comfortable in groups so I liked it best when it was just the two of us—me and my best friend (whichever friend I was with at the time). I was probably a difficult best friend, because I wanted no secrets, no darkness between us.

When I first met Billy, I felt the same way. I wanted to know all of him and to be honest with him about everything about myself. It drove him crazy for me to dig at him, to get at his true feelings, and after the first few years, I quit trying. Billy liked to talk about his dreams, but I soon realized that's all they were, just dreams, because he never intended to act on them.

I quit dreaming a long time ago because I realized I didn't have a clue how to make them come true. Once I admitted to myself that I was married to a drunk, my only goal in life was survival and escape for myself and my children. I guess I haven't done the job all that well since we don't seem to be any better off financially. I'm no great success at what I do, and some nights I get so lonely I think I'll scream. Then I remember life with a drunk and I know that I have succeeded, no matter how small the success. I have risen above.

The train chugged noisily, alternately disappearing and reappearing as it negotiated the many tunnels that sewed the folds of the mountains together. It was a motion of endless curves, winding, meandering ever deeper into the lush green hills. The heavy stream of white smoke that it belched out behind hung heavily in the still morning air, and suddenly with a burst of downhill speed, it rattled loudly and charged through a tunnel and out into the valley along the river's edge. The morning sun was barely peeping over the highest mountain folds and the morning fog from the small river parted slowly to reveal the rows of nearly identical houses that sat along its edge. All looked serene and peaceful, surreal almost as the fog lifted from this tiny coal mining camp town.

But all too soon, the sun's rays would dissipate the fog and the grayness, in all of its ugly reality, would be revealed, the poverty, the loneliness and sameness of life in this hidden little town; a town that supported no businesses any more; just homes and churches—some of those abandoned as well—all overlaid with a layer of grime and the grayness of the coal dust that permeated everything. The train pulled empty coal cars that bounced and jostled noisily along the tracks as the train made its way back to the tipple to be refilled, and then they would be on their way again. Off to the cities and power plants far from these green mountains. Energy for factories and manufacturing that had been dug from the bowels of the earth.

Tess snuggled deeper into the blankets as the train approached; visualizing its passage in and out of the tunnels, as the sound alternately grew and then faded as it made its way over the myriad of tracks that looked as if a giant needle had stitched them into the side of the mountain. Her "twin" and best friend, Teresa from next door, had spent the night and she could hear the soft sounds of her breathing; her blond hair lying across her face, one hand tucked beneath her chin. She still slumbered deep in her dreams.

It was still early morning and they had stayed up much too late the night before, but it was Saturday so they could sleep in as long as they wanted. Her mom had gone out to a little beer joint with friends to listen to a local band the night before and Teresa had stayed with her, as she often did, so she didn't have to be alone. She didn't like staying in the little house alone at night. She hoped her mom hadn't brought her boyfriend home with her. It made her uncomfortable to be around her mom's many boyfriends, but Teresa helped; Teresa could make her laugh at just about anything.

After Daddy died, she and Momma had moved back to Virginia and into one of the small row houses that made up this old mining camp town, built in the bottom along the river's edge. It had two small bedrooms and one bath, probably no more than a thousand square feet in the entire house. But no one noticed. All of the houses were exactly the same except for paint colors or small modifications made to the floor plan inside. Flanked by the river and the train tracks in back and a highway in front, there was little land or yard space; just enough for a few dusty flowers in front and a small garden in back.

Bombarded by the constant sounds of coal trucks passing by on one side and the trains on the other, it would have seemed to be a miserable situation, but the occupants of the houses were used to the noise, to the rumbles of the trains or the rattles of the big trucks, just as they were used to the dust and the grayness from the layers of coal dust that colored everything in their world. Coal was the bread and butter in this area, the staff of life. Without the coal, there were no jobs. So when the trains and the trucks stopped running, it meant hard times had come.

A finger of light slid over the top of a mountain fold sending shafts of warm sunlight down into the valley, and just for a moment caught in its golden beam, the beauty and the strength of the people below was reflected. Their hopes and dreams, the same as those of families everywhere—a good life, home, family, good times—but they are buried beneath the poverty, beneath years of struggle and pain, beneath the fear of change and the fear of loss buried within the layers of coal dust.

# Daddy's Girl

April 14, 19??

I want to write a story with real life in it, something that gives a glimpse of the hard side of life. So far I haven't been able to do this. Most things I write only tell the events or are in "storybook" form, taken from good things that have happened. Even at the age of fourteen, I know life has both a good side and a bad side. So I am going to try, hopefully not in vain, to put my actual feelings on paper.

April 4 was just another day to most people, but for me, it held special meaning. For on this day I turned fourteen! And I awoke to a special treat—snow! I loved the cold freshness the snow seemed to give to everything, making the air seem so pure. Lovely, but cold, but with snow, who minds the cold? Especially at fourteen! So that morning, I raced out sockless and hatless but heart full to meet the day. I received Happy Birthday greetings from friends and even a few presents and cards, but the best gift of all was from Mother Nature, the snow. I loved walking up town to the post office after school, running and laughing all alone in a world of whiteness!

But now, not even two weeks later, everything has changed. The snow is gone and nothing beautiful is left.

I'll try to explain as I sit here, shivering from the cold and for some reason, with tears in my eyes. It's only eight o'clock, and I am home alone. Mom's out with friends—including her latest boyfriend—and I am here alone as Teresa couldn't stay with me tonight. The furnace isn't working, so my only heat is from an electric heater and it's not doing a very good job. My kitten and my puppy are sleeping besides me as I write and all is quiet except for the passing cars on the road outside and the soft sounds of their breathing.

Thinking on life, at times it's a breeze when there are good moments that seem so grand, right out of a book. And I should know as I read lots of books. But good moments seem to be so few, and instead, there are bad times that seem so cold, a cruel cold, not like the fresh whiteness of the snow. Like when Daddy died, I wanted to cry and cry and cry, but my siblings told me not to for Mom's sake, that it would upset her to see me cry. So I held it all in but I know now I shouldn't have. I feel like I never had the chance to grieve; it all became a blur, the funeral, the crowds of friends and relatives, neighbors bringing food, the flowers and fruit baskets, and then before long I was back in school. But my whole world had changed and I wanted the other kids to know, to give me understanding and sympathy. But we lived near Detroit when he died, and these were the kids who had teased me about my accent and called me Hillbilly. And even though my daddy had died and I was grieving, nothing had changed. I was still just that shy little girl with the terrible hillbilly accent. It hurt, I felt deprived, like I was missing out on something. I wanted them to care, to show support. I guess this was an important lesson on life.

And then my world changed again. Mom started to go out a lot with friends, and then she started to date sometimes. Most of the time, it was just the two of us at home, especially once Becca finished college and then got married and moved away, so Mom depended on me. I feel like I grew up overnight, at such an early age. All I wanted was to be loved, understood, taken care of, but no one ever asked what I wanted or needed. Instead, they told me how things would be, where we would live, where I would go to school. And I just had to accept it and be there when they needed me. And I was, I am, I try to give with all the wisdom I have. I try to be cheerful, I try to meet their needs, give them what they need to see in me, just like I did when I was little. But inside, I feel so shy and insecure and yet far older and wiser than anyone realizes.

My life seems to be divided into two parts—Before Daddy Died and After Daddy Died. Before, I tagged along with him whenever he would let me. We shared chocolate covered peanuts and he called me his water boy when I carried water to him in the fields. After, I missed him and I still need him…but he isn't here anymore, so I can't have him.

Now my thoughts switch to Ricky. We had a sock hop last night and both Ricky and I were there. We danced, a lot. It feels so nice when he kisses me and I want to be loved, but I won't have sex with him. I'm too young for that, and my family thinks too highly of me, I think too highly of me, to do that.

I pray a lot and I go to church pretty often. I need a father figure to watch over me. I know I could be wild if I wanted to. I have always been such a good little girl that Mom trusts me, so she lets me go just about anywhere I want. But I have a very tight hold on myself. Sometimes I'm afraid if I let go, I would have a nervous breakdown. I don't want that and I don't want to be wild. Instead I want to get an education and do something great. Maybe become a freelance photographer or something like that. Not so that mom can say she raised me right, but because of my own pride.

I get angry when people say I look like my mom. I wanted to scream, "I do not!" I don't want to look like my mom; I want to look like my dad. He had deep set pale blue eyes with bushy brows and sandy brown hair. I sometimes try to imagine my life if he hadn't died. I can't say if it would have been really different or not. Maybe I was destined to lose my Father, but I just wish he was here to help me sometimes with the growing up stuff. Life seems really hard when you feel there's no one to turn to. I don't talk to my mom; she has enough worries just trying to make ends meet. And to most others in my family, I'm just a kid. So what kind of problems could I have? Well, let's see, there's boys and drugs and sex and dating, drinking and parties. No, nothing at all to worry about, just the usual stuff.

Becca tells me not to grow old and bitter and to remember that the world owes me nothing no matter how hard my life is. She's the one who suggested I write when I get upset or angry at the world. She says that she feels bitter sometimes and because of this, she unconsciously takes revenge on other people at times. I know how that feels. I have had days where I wanted to take revenge too. On those days, I only allowed the people closest to me to speak to me but anyone else received either no reply or a smart assed reply. I called those my person "not people days," meaning that I chose to associate with a few persons, but not people in general. I know how wrong that was, "people" hadn't done anything to hurt me, and in fact, maybe I was hurting myself by pushing them away.

How strange that I didn't know I had such insight until I saw those words on paper. Maybe Becca's right about writing this stuff down. Or maybe I just stumbled onto an answer.

Last night, Ricky and I were dancing to a slow song and he pulled me to him and started kissing me. *So nice.* I wish it was the real thing but of course it's not, and eventually it will only lead to hurt. I want no more of that. I think I've had my fair share for a lifetime. But I know that's impossible. I know more hurtful things will come.

I'm sure a lot of people would read that and think, "What a nut!" But I'm not hard to understand. I'm just me, a person. A living breathing soul, put here by God. What I do with this life now is up to me. I just feel so alone.

This little kitten will never have to worry about food or shelter; it will always have someone to take care of it. Little children are like that. No problems, no worries about tomorrow. But then tomorrow comes and the child grows. That's the sad part—the child grows and learns about the bad things, the hard things, and the child loses its innocence.

I think autumn is my favorite season. My father died in the fall, so most people would say that should be my least favorite. But everything dies in autumn, even my father, but nature leaves behind a bright promise of spring, a time of newness, new beginnings. Like the promise of my father within me. So when autumn comes and the leaves start to fall, I remember that Daddy is gone but I'm still here, so let's see what I can do. It gives me fresh hope and courage even though everything in nature is dying.

I'm tired and would like to go to sleep. Perhaps I might even dream about Ricky. By the way, sometimes I have dreams that come true. Honest. I dream the future. I don't remember them until they happen and it's usually just a little snippet, a picture only almost. It's uncanny, such a feeling of déjà vu! The first time it happened was in the summer before Daddy died. It was very brief, just a fleeting picture, but now sometimes, the dreams are longer. I even dream what I'm supposed to say or what others are saying. I usually change what I'm supposed to say just to change the course of things in case it's a premonition of losing someone again.

I just heard a noise in the kitchen! I hope it's just the momma cat. I always get so scared here alone at night. I went and got my pistol from Momma's wardrobe. I feel a little better now. I'd like to stop writing, the mood has broken anyway, I can't think of what else to say.

I just picked up this gun and I looked at it. Without pulling back the hammer or putting my finger anywhere near the trigger, I held it up to my head and I thought, *I could pull this trigger and kill myself, I could leave this diary as a farewell note to Mom and then I wouldn't be alone anymore.*

But then I thought, *No, never.* I cherish life more than anything and I fear death so much, so I know I am by no means ready to face it. So I put the gun down and picked my pen back up. Maybe the moral of this rambling is "write, don't shoot!" HA!

Veteran's Hospital
Admission 4/1/19??
Discharge 4/26/19??

This 46 year old, married, WWII veteran was re-admitted to this hospital on April 1, 196?, with a history of over-indulgence in alcohol for the past four months and possible D.T.'s. He has two previous admissions to this hospital and was first admitted here in November 196? on the Medical Service and treated for acute and chronic alcoholism with convulsive disorder. Most recent admission occurred in June 196? for essentially the same trouble and he was discharged after twenty-four in-patient days.

Chief complaint: "Got to drinking a whole lot, so sick I thought I would die." The patient said he had been drinking since January 1, consuming approximately a case of beer per day plus a half a gallon of moonshine. Subsequently he became sick in the stomach, started being nauseated and vomiting and he reports to have vomited some blood prior to admission. He entered this hospital on the advice of his family since he was "just about to die." Apparently there was some quarreling and aggravation going on at home as a result of his drinking. The patient admits that it is all his fault. Since his last hospitalization he had not been steadily employed and has been doing odd chores around the house and subsidizing on social security and on a government pension. In the years past he admits to have fabricated some moonshine liquor for himself. His last job was working in the coal mines approximately three years ago. Patient admits to not sleeping well while drinking and since on his last spree has had "foolish dreams – seeing snakes," but he denies hearing voices. He has felt sad and discouraged but has no plans to commit suicide. He feels life is worth living and there is "no hurry to leave." He has never attended AA meetings but is ready to consider this now. It appears that the patient's condition is now about the same as it was on his last admission. He displays a coarse tremor of his extremities, is rather sluggish in talking and movements and displays an unsteady gait.

When interviewed by the case physician, he stated that three years ago he got his back hurt in the mines. He tried to work after this but couldn't. He had a spinal fusion of his back. He is considered totally and permanently disabled by the Veterans. He drew social security for two years until he tried to work then the social security was stopped even though he could not work. Since his last admission his father has died. He was ninety-five years old. His mother is sixty-six and she looked after his father until his death. The patient plans to go home and help with the garden, watch TV and read when he leaves the hospital. He says he drinks for the effect, but he doesn't want it if he leaves off the first drink. He stated that he did not go to AA while in the hospital.

Physical examination by the admitting doctor showed a scar in the epigastrium from a gastrectomy. Six inch long scar over the lumbosacral area and a four inch scar over the sacral area. Flexion is limited. Ten inch scar anterior aspect of the right calf. Fine tremor of the hands. Routine laboratory work on admission was within limits of normal. X-ray of the chest was normal. His tonometry was within normal limits on the second testing.

While in the hospital the patient was treated with Thorazine. Later this was changed to Librium, 50 mgm. q.i.d. and i.m. when necessary, and was reduced to 25 mgm. q.i.d. It was later reduced to twice daily. The patient was discharged on Librium, 25 mgm. He was considered competent. The patient was also given Lederplex, 1 capsule b.i.d. for 5 days.

# THE NEED TO BE LOVED

"I see it Mom! Look, there it is!" Sammy tugged at Tess's arm, eagerly pointing to the big dipper hanging in the dark expanse of sky. His breath created white puffs as he spoke and Tess snuggled him close as she too stared up at the heavens.

It had been a good day. They'd had a nice family Thanksgiving dinner, just the six of them. Of course, Gina had stopped by unexpectedly to join them for dessert. Although Tess suspected it was for moral support to Tressa when she had dropped the bombshell that she'd been asked by Bob's mom to model in the holiday fashion show in two weeks. Gina had clapped and cheered, leaving little doubt she thought it was a good idea.

Tressa had been showing her strength in not only helping out at the photo studio after school, but she occasionally worked at Bob's salon as a receptionist as well. Bob frequently sang her praises telling Tess that Tressa was brilliant. She'd not only revamped the files at Posterity, but at Bob's salon as well. She had created a computerized database that stored even more client information for both locations and had updated the search process to pull up results faster.

Bob had taken her to his mom's studio to set up a similar system, and his mom had instantly fallen in love with Tressa's self-confidence and poise. She had offered her free modeling sessions in exchange for her assistance with updating the computerized client information, which Tressa had eagerly accepted. Tess worried that even that modest "dabbling" in the modeling world would fill her head with dreams of fame and money, and Tressa was petite, certainly not the typical 5'10" model. She didn't want her to be disappointed that she was never going to be on the cover of a magazine.

But today, Tressa had laid those fears to rest and surprised all of them when she explained that she'd accepted the classes as well as the chance to model, just to learn more about the business because that was the area she was really interested in—the business aspect. She wanted to learn all she could about all three businesses—four if you counted Uncle Grant's business—in fact, she was doing a school paper on the marketing aspects of shared information and client lists between each business and the impact it could have on the overall bottom line for all. She had decided she wanted to work in marketing and find ways to grow their client lists; her head was filled with advertising and marketing ideas and they were all stunned at her enthusiasm as she tossed out various scenarios from joint commercials to shared mass mail marketing ideas.

Tess was surprised to learn that she had already been talking to Uncle Grant and to Bob and his mother about her ideas, and even more surprised to learn that Bob had encouraged her to think about a marketing degree.

"So," Tressa said, picking at the crust of the cherry pie on her plate with the tip of her fork, "I think I would like to do dual enrollment next year in school, and definitely in my senior year. That way I can earn college credits and get a jump start on my requirements for college." Tess was so stunned she thought she would fall off of her chair. Before she could formulate her thoughts to make a reply, Tressa continued.

"Of course, I want to keep working part-time for you, Mom, and for Bob and Ms. Kirkenbaum, and maybe for you too, Uncle Grant. I can get a good marketing degree from the community college, and I'll take some additional classes online." She shrugged and Tess noticed Grant nodding his head and Patty smiling so big it looked as if her jaws would break.

"I'm not looking to be a big city advertiser; I just want to be good at marketing here in our own little area in our own businesses." Tess didn't fail to notice the use of the word "our" and she noticed Grant's smile grew wide at her choice of words. Was this her child? Had she really changed so much in such a few short weeks? Or had she herself just failed to listen closely to what Tressa had been saying all along?

Tressa added that Ms. Kirkenbaum had told her that if Tess agreed, she could continue to help out part-time in any of the businesses that might need her and she could save money to pay for classes. "It won't be like going away for college, but that's okay. I'm a hometown girl anyway, and it'll be more fun this way, I'll get to dabble in marketing in the businesses I love while I'm learning!" She shrugged her shoulders again, and smiled at her mother. "Provided you agree, of course."

*Agree?* Tess had thought with a mental shake of her head, *Of course she would agree. Her daughter had found something she enjoyed, something she was good at. She had found her focus. What was there to disagree with?*

Tess jumped jolted back to the present when Tressa gently touched her cheek with icy fingers. "It's too cold out here for me, I'm going back inside!" She watched as her daughter tugged the sliding glass door open and hurried back into Grant's warm dining room. They had finished dinner hours ago, and everyone had been sitting around, watching football and sampling desserts since. She'd eaten so much she felt sluggish, but content; Tressa's news had put warmth in her heart that even the cold air couldn't seem to take away.

She pulled Sammy's hood up over his ears, remembering how she had loved the crisp coldness of autumn as a child. She remembered sitting out on the porch for hours, just watching the cars go by, until her cheeks and fingers and toes were numb, before relenting and going inside. "Can you find the little dipper?" she asked, although she couldn't remember if it was even visible at this time of year.

As Sam perused the skies, she turned to smile at Grant as he exited the house behind them, telescope in hand. "Let's see if we can find the old man in the moon, Sam," he said. After carefully adjusting the legs of the scopes tripod, he pointed it to the skies.

"Remember when you asked if we could watch the astronauts on the moon with this thing?" he asked Tess.

Laughing, she asked, "Have you really had that thing that long?"

Grant nodded. "Yup, it was one of my first purchases when I started making money. You and I used to put in a lot of hours with this thing."

"I never did get to see those astronauts though."

"Did you watch it on TV, Mom?" Sam asked.

"Did she ever," Grant answered for her. "She stayed glued to the television for days every time there was a moon shot. She swore she wanted to be an astronaut."

"Why didn't you, Mom?"

"Well, for one thing, I discovered I was afraid of heights!" She gave him a lopsided smile. "And then my science teacher told me how many different types of math and sciences I would need to study and that kind of changed my mind. Those subjects were never my favorite. And my guidance counselor told me that girls couldn't be astronauts anyway."

"They can too! Girls can be anything they want."

"That's a good attitude, Sam. But when I was a young girl, things were a lot different. And in the small town where I grew up, girls weren't encouraged to go to college or to plan for careers." She smiled and ruffled his hair. "Besides, if I had become an astronaut I might not have become your mommy!"

"Here, son, take a look." Grant guided Sam as he peered through the telescope and Tess smiled watching the two of them together. Grant had shown the same kind of patience when she was young, but she had been shy around him; he had gone away to college when she was still a small child and by the time he returned, she'd been an adolescent and things had changed so much she hadn't known what to say to him anymore. Grant had never been overly comfortable with words anyway, so he would be silent as long as she was, but when she had needed to talk, he had always tried to be there. She knew it was important for children to not only have someone listen to them but to have someone who was comfortable talking and sharing with them as well, so she tried hard to never make any subject taboo with her own kids. Though they seemed to hate it, she frequently attempted to initiate conversations on difficult subjects, not that they shared much with her, usually rolling their eyes at how "out of touch" she was instead, but still she worked hard to keep the lines of communication open.

*Please, let it be enough*, she thought, turning her eyes skyward. She had given thanks earlier for the blessing of her children. Without them, her life would be empty. *Just please, let them grow up to be good people with bright futures.* She mentally added to her silent prayer.

"How's the new venture going?" Grant asked suddenly, shaking her from her reverie.

"Remarkably well; we're booked full for the next week with sittings ranging from an hour to half a day, depending on what the customer wants. Most of them, the bookings are in the studio but some are at locations around town, parks, and historical sites. If we book any more, I'm going to have to add a photographer and another assistant. As it is, we're going to add to our Saturday hours and keep the studio open all day. We're even going to add specialized Sunday hours, by reservation only for photo shoots."

She shook her head. "I wasn't sure what the demand would be, but I guess Posterity's reputation combined with Bob's marketing efforts is creating instant popularity." As she said the words, she realized where Tressa's interest in marketing had developed. She'd been helping Bob on several of his projects, and she had smiled watching their heads bent together over some advertising layout. But she hadn't been paying close enough attention as she had failed to see how much Tressa enjoyed it. "Even some of our oldest customers have expressed an interest in outdoor portraits. They like the idea of receiving the photos electronically" she continued, turning her attention back to Grant. "Some have even told me to tell Ross it was about time he got on board with the new way of doing things!"

"What does Bob think about all the success?" Grant asked, having not failed to notice her casual use of the other man's first name.

"He's not as surprised as Gina and I are. He said he expected it to be a hit, but he is a little surprised at how quickly it happened!"

"Have you told Ross yet?" Tess got a brief glimpse of Grant's face in the lighter's flare as he lit one of the small, aromatic cigars he occasionally enjoyed smoking. The rich aroma teased her nose and reminded her of the long rides around the countryside in his jeep that they had taken when she was a young girl. Patty hated the fragrance of the small, square cut cigars, and chased him away whenever he wanted to light up, but the smell was nostalgic to her.

"Not yet," she sighed, "I am waiting to close the books at the end of the month. When you get me the cash flow report to take with me, I will tell him what I've done. So make sure you show a fantastic profit for me." She teased, then she grimaced. "Of course, I may have to plead for charity when he fires me!"

"He's not going to fire you, not if the figures look good. In fact, if he's smart, he'll give you a big fat Christmas bonus." Grant took a deep draw from his cigar. "And if he does, I expect a great Christmas present from you!" He chuckled, tapping her on the end of her nose as if she were still the baby niece he'd once taken care of.

"Mom," Sam's teeth chattered as he interrupted their conversation, "is the flag that Buzz Alderman and Neil Armstrong put on the moon still there?"

"Buzz Aldrin," she corrected, "and I'm not sure, but we are going inside now before you catch pneumonia and get to spend the next week home from school."

"I wouldn't mind. In fact, I'm gonna stay out here all night, I'll even take my coat off!" Sam grinned and unzipped his coat, pushing back against her as she playfully swatted his rear and strong armed him inside. Grant gently tugged her back before she could follow Sam, and she turned expectantly to see if he needed her help with something.

But he turned his back to her as he casually re-folded the legs of the tripod. "Patty told me she saw you having lunch with Bob a couple of weeks ago. She saw the two of you going into the Potter's Cottage."

Tess silently seethed inside but just nodded politely and replied, "Yes, he took me and Gina out to celebrate the day we sealed the deal on the trial period of the new venture. It seemed like a silly idea to me, but Gina was so excited, I went along."

Grant stared at her thoughtfully in the darkness for a moment before nodding and tossing the stub of the cigar out onto the damp lawn.

"Patty will have you out there tomorrow picking that up," she teased as he pulled the door open and motioned her in ahead of him.

"Not if you don't tell."

Tess laughed. "She'll see it anyway, but I'll keep my mouth shut as long as there's something in it for me."

Grant rolled his eyes skyward as they tugged out of their coats. "Sheesh, women! Why do we men think we gotta have 'em in our lives? Why do we think we gotta be loved? We're big boys. We don't need someone telling us not to eat too much ice cream or watch too much TV!"

"Don't give me that, you'd be lucky to remember to wash your socks if Patty wasn't here to do it for you!" She playfully punched him in the arm, feeling a stab of envy at the closeness she knew Grant and Patty still shared even after so many years of marriage. It felt sometimes as if she'd always been alone. Of course, togetherness took openness and she'd gotten to be an expert at holding things inside. Could she ever open up again, let someone share her innermost fears and thoughts?

Unbidden, Bob's handsome face floated into her mind and she flushed to think she'd associated him with her thoughts. He had such soulful brown eyes, so kind and tender at times when he looked at her. *Pity*, she thought, *he feels pity and here I am trying to picture him as a lifelong partner.* Of course, that thought led to thoughts of all that a marriage meant including sharing a bed and her face flared hotter. Thankful for the dim lighting in the now empty dining room, she tossed her jacket onto the back of a chair and made her escape to the bathroom.

Turning the tap in the sink, she splashed her cheeks with cold water and stared at her reflection in the mirror as she patted her face dry. She slowly shook her head; she didn't seem to know what she wanted from life anymore and she didn't like this emptiness inside, the loneliness she felt. Grant's words turned in her head, *Why do we think we gotta be loved?* And with a flash of insight she knew that was it, that was what she wanted—she wanted to be loved. She wanted to come first in someone's life; she wanted to be cherished just once.

She wanted someone to care about her, to care whether she was happy or content. Someone she could share her days with, her thoughts, her hopes and plans. Someone she could care about in return. Was that too much to ask? Shouldn't everyone have that in their lives? That she couldn't answer. She only knew that love, real love, had never been hers and just once she would like to experience it.

She was jarred from her thoughts by a knock at the door. "Mom? Are you in there?" Tressa called through the door. "Do you wanna play Uno with us?"

Turning off the tap, she refolded the tea towel and called back, "Sure honey, that sounds great. I'll be right out."

# SHADOWS

November 28

The kids and I put the Christmas decorations up at the shop today with Gina's help. We made a fun day of it; we had popcorn and hot chocolate and played Christmas carols while we worked. Gina has been such a lifesaver and she is so happy with the new project; I have my fingers crossed it will continue to succeed. And I hope financially, Ross can give her a good bonus this year. We're starting new holiday hours tomorrow and we have another radio AD coming out. I can't believe how successful those ads have been.

    Meanwhile, I keep putting off the inevitable, but I know that soon I have to tell Ross about our new venture. I want to have the end-of-the-month financial figures to show him first though; I think (hope) he'll be pleased. Even with Bob's cut, I think we should still see a good return. I haven't really put up any capital from the shop, just mine and Gina's time, and she volunteered to assist with the setup off the clock just to get the opportunity. If he's unhappy, I guess we can just shut it all down, no loss except for Gina's pride. (And mine!)

But I can't think of work or the shop any more tonight. My thoughts keep turning inward; I keep seeing snippets of things from the past, wondering why I didn't pay more attention to them then. Like all of the different guys who flirted with me, even a few who professed their love for me, and somehow I still ended up with Billy. I truly believe it had very little to do with rational thought. I liked Billy; I still do. He is a sweet man who loves being liked by everyone.

I think he felt nonthreatening. He moved slowly, he didn't push for sex right away, and I was lonely; I needed someone to hold onto, and someone to save. Someone to replace the father I couldn't save, I suppose. For whatever reason, I think children of alcoholics are drawn to addictive personalities. I think I sensed that in Billy from the very beginning, and that's why I clung to him for so long.

It seems illogical when I look back now. We are so different in so many ways. He loves to party and to be in crowds. Me, I've always been content being alone, and when I entertain, I like being with my family or close friends, not large groups of people I hardly know. Billy likes the wild life while I've always tried to avoid it. I like order and a peaceful home life. I like quiet dinners or going to see a show; I like plays, concerts, watching a ballgame. Billy likes smoky bars and overly made up women, dirty jokes, and loud, bawdy laughter. I like reading, going for walks, and taking pictures of the kids, nature, sunsets. If Billy takes a walk, there better be a beer at the end of it. In the beginning though, I ignored our differences. I thought they didn't matter or that I could change him. I guess it was the typical "good girl/bad boy" marriage—doomed to fail.

I was lonely and insecure when I met Billy. During my early teen years, I hit a growth spurt, and suddenly my legs had seemed too long for my body. I felt awkward and gawky; taller than all the tiny, petite females in my family I found myself stooping or slouching whenever

I was around them. Subconsciously, I think I associated being pretty and feminine with being petite, and though I'm no giant, my growth spurt stopped at 5'3", but all the other women in my family are 5' and under. I have a long inseam for my small frame, and I know now that doesn't make me a freak. But at fourteen, I just felt gawky and ugly. It was a long, long time before I felt attractive again, and although when I look at old photographs I can see what a pretty young woman I was, at the time I just felt ugly and uncoordinated.

It was during this time that I met Billy, and I suppose the fact that at first he just talked to me was what drew me to him. Besides feeling tall and awkward, I was a straight A student and spent lots of time with my nose stuck in a book, which put most guys off. If they paid attention to me, it was just to try and cheat from my papers in class or find a quiet spot to try and cop a feel of my chest, which had spurted along with my legs. Their attentions did nothing to help my self-confidence. I knew you didn't have to be pretty for a guy to want to do "it" with you; you just had to have boobs.

I wanted someone to talk to, someone to be friends with before they tried to cop a feel, and along came Billy. In spite of his wildness, Billy is used to being around women; he has four older sisters, so he can easily talk about topics women like. He's also a very intelligent, kind person, although he tries to hide the intelligence most of the time. And Billy can talk to anyone, from a druggie in a bar to a congressman at a campaign rally, and afterwards both would remember what a nice guy he was. Easygoing and likable, that's Billy.

It was a long time before I realized that was all that Billy did, just talk. All the dreams he told me about, all the things he wanted to have some day, they were all just that, just dreams. They were things he wanted but was never going to put forth any effort to actually achieve them. Billy likes to take it easy. He likes to complain about how unfair things are, but he does nothing to try and change them. I'm glad he doesn't bother to try and come and visit the kids too often. Of course, he doesn't bother with child support too often either, but at least he doesn't confuse them with all of his talk, all of his pipe dreams.

He has plenty of girlfriends to share his dreams with, he's never been lonely that way; he draws women like honey draws flies. That was another thing that soon went wrong in our marriage, it was impossible to trust him. He slept with my friends, his boss' wives; everyone seemed to want to sleep with Billy. It got so bad that I never knew if the mothers of the kid's friends came by to chat with me or to try and catch him home alone.

It took me a long time to figure this out though. At first, I just thought I had found love. I thought I had found someone to talk to, to share my life with; someone who wouldn't go away as it seemed my entire family had done. I was very lonely after my siblings and Uncle Grant left home, and Billy filled that empty space. Unfortunately, I chose to ignore the fact that he wasn't as content to sit home alone with me as I was with him.

Incompatibility, the judge called it. It took a long time for me to see that he wasn't ever going to change; he didn't want to settle down. I thought there was nothing that love couldn't overcome but I was missing one important factor, Billy didn't really love me. I think he loved having me there to look after him, to keep house and cook his meals. A place he could come home to when he was tired of partying, someone to come and get him when he was too drunk to drive home. He wanted a combination of a sister/mother figure, but not a wife, not a partner, just someone who would be there when he needed them. But he wasn't in love with me. He never even really knew me.

## SHADOWS

Shadows move in and out of my life
Remembered faces
Remembered emotions
Flickering in the firelight

Shadows dance against my lids
Some are real
Some are figments of my dreams
That never came true

And you, you are the shadow
That I most longed to hold
But you faded with the sunrise
Leaving only prisms of light
Reflected in my mind

Shadows of what might have been
But will never be
Fading softly into the photo album
Of my heart
Where all shadow dreams live

S. Smith

History and Physical
Patient admitted by his wife on 7/7/196?
Complaint: Pain to shoulder and right hand
History:

This patient came to the emergency room on the night of the 7th of July complaining of pain in his right shoulder and right hand and the right hand was swollen. The patient apparently had been drinking for 2 days and apparently had scuffled with someone and fell down and injured himself, although he seemed unsure of exactly what occurred. *(The truth was that he had fallen from our 2nd story porch, the railing was being replaced and he went out to relieve himself from the porch instead of using the restroom and had fallen over the side, he made up the story of the scuffle as a cover)*. X-Rays were obtained and showed a complete fracture of the right clavicle and a fracture of the 3rd and 4th metacarpals of his right hand in fair position.

PH:

Reveals the patient had been operated on for ulcers in his stomach four years ago and apparently has not had much trouble with this. He still continues to drink.

Physical examination:
Revealed a well developed, well nourished, 47 year old man with acute injuries of the right hand and shoulder.

Head and neck – the eyes were quite red and blood shot. He had some slight abrasions about the face which were not significant.

Heart – blood pressure 160/90.

Lungs – clear to auscultation.

Trunk – negative except for the right shoulder where there was a palpable fracture in the right clavicle.

Abdomen – seemed normal.

Extremities – there was swelling and tenderness in the right hand.

Impression:

Displaced fracture of the right clavicle, slightly comminuted. Fracture of the 3rd and 4th metacarpals of the right hand.

T.J. Penn, M.D.

Clinical Summary					Admitted 7/7/196?
								Discharged 7/9/196?

Course in hospital:

This patient was admitted by Dr. Gomez to my service with the history as recorded.

Laboratory work:

Hematocrit 50, hemoglobin 14.00, white count 16,0000 with 81 polys and 19 lymphs. Urine showed 1.020 specific gravity, negative albumin, negative sugar, 6 to 8 white cells, 2 to 3 white cells and 1+ bacteria.

On the 7th of July I saw the patient and applied a clavicle splint for the fracture of the clavicle and did a splint dressing for the fractures in the hand. He was given Talwin for pain, diet was allowed. He had an uneventful course and was discharged on July 9th and will be followed in the office.

Final Diagnosis:

Fracture of the clavicle, right.
Fracture of the 3rd and 4th metacarpals, right.

Operation:

Application of clavicle splint for fracture of clavicle. Splint dressing for fractures of the 3rd and 4th metacarpals, right hand.

T. J. Penn, M.D.

# SHADES OF GRAY

Tess nervously chewed at the soft flesh on the inside of her lower lip as she watched the cold December rain run in rivulets down the wide picture window overlooking Ross's front yard. Puddles were gathering in the low spots from the heavy consistent downpour that had been falling since before daybreak and the yard looked cold and dismal, which did nothing to soothe her jangled nerves. This area of Virginia had mild winters that were often more rain with overcast gray days than snow and ice, which could at times make them seem longer and harsher than the cold and snow she had experienced as a child growing up farther west in the mountains. There, at least, the sun came out after the snow fell and made it seem a little less gloomy than the endless grayness that often accompanied winters here so close to the Tidewater area.

She'd picked up the balance sheets and the end of month statements from Grant's office first thing that morning and made the drive out to Ross's house. After listening to her discuss all that she'd been doing at the shop, he had taken the profit and loss statements and other reports and gone into his home office, leaving her to pace the soft carpeted floor of his large family room as she waited, unconsciously jingling the car keys in her pocket.

It worried her that he'd remained silent throughout her explanation on the new venture, showing no emotion as he listened. Becky had been quick to assure him that Tess had only proceeded with her blessing, but he'd only nodded, seemingly brushing her words aside. Then, after asking her to wait while he reviewed the accounting statements, he'd disappeared, saying they'd talk more when he was done.

Becky had brought Tess a cup of coffee which now sat cold and untouched on an end table, the cream congealed into an unappetizing ring at the top, and after an attempt to engage her in small talk, Becky had discreetly left her alone to nervously pace the floor while she waited. Fear tightened in the center of Tess' chest like a fist. Ross had been good to her. How could she have been so bold with his business? He'd taught her everything and she'd repaid him by playing a wild card with his livelihood! She wouldn't blame him if he were mad at her.

"Well, you have been a busy lady!" Ross spoke so suddenly from the doorway behind her that Tess jumped and turned quickly to face him. Becky stood at his side, her wide smile reassuring, even as Ross's tone sounded stern.

"I didn't want you to worry during your recovery; I wanted things to be business as usual."

"Well"—Ross tapped the papers in his hand against his leg, and her heart sank at his next words—"I don't think it was exactly business as usual." He held the end of month statements up and tapped them in the air. "I would say instead that you did that and then some from the looks of these." The smile that suddenly lit his face drew the tension from her body as surely and as suddenly as if he'd flipped a switch. "And I just can't say thank you enough! Come here you. What would Becky and I do without you?" He opened his arms wide and drew her into a great bear hug. She could sense the emotion coursing through his body as he gently patted her back. Releasing her, he cleared his throat as Becky stepped forward to hug her as well.

"We are both so grateful," Becky told her, planting a soft kiss on her cheek. "You have been like a daughter to us and we want you to know it has not gone unnoticed." Becky stepped back and held out an envelope. "Here's a little gift to you. Consider it your year-end bonus and our thank-you wrapped into one."

"And, we wanted to let you know,"—Ross smiled at Becky as he spoke—"we've decided to make you a partner in Posterity, going forth from the date of my heart attack. You'll retain your full salary, plus a generous pay raise that you'll find outlined in the paperwork attached to your bonus, plus each quarter you'll get a percentage of the profit. I think you'll find the numbers satisfactory, but by all means have Grant look them over. I plan to make Bob a partner in this new venture as well and of course, you will be a full partner in that as well. That is, if you say yes."

Tess realized her mouth must be hanging open and she swallowed hard and mumbled her thank-you, "I…um…thank you both so much. I don't know what to say."

Becky chuckled. "Just say yes; unless of course, you want some time to think it over."

"And maybe, a 'thank you' boss is in order?" Ross teased.

Tess laughed. "Yes, of course, thank you boss, and yes, of course it's yes!" She hugged them both again and soon they were all seated at the kitchen table, enjoying a slice of Becky's gingerbread with fresh brewed coffee.

Before she left, Becky reminded her of the holiday party they were giving for employees and friends later in the month. "Semi-formal this year. We have a lot to celebrate, and I plan to do it up spectacular! Maybe even have it catered," Becky had told her. "And I expect you to use some of that money to buy a gorgeous new outfit to wear!"

Heading back to town she found it hard to concentrate on her driving, but the narrow back roads and dismal weather demanded her attention. Her head swam with happiness and disbelief, and she realized she still hadn't looked at the check Becky had given her. Sighing, she gave into temptation and pulled onto the shoulder of the road. Throwing the car into park, she pulled the envelope from her bag and quickly broke the seal. Taking a deep breath, she pulled out the Christmas card and other papers that were tucked inside, the check sliding out from the center and into her lap. But she deliberately averted her eyes and opened the card first, taking the time to read the sweet words of thanks and praise that Ross had written inside the card in his own hand; her eyes welling with tears, she smiled at the humorous, tongue-in-cheek tone of his message, in which he teased that with such a spectacular boss, how could she be anything but great.

Finally, drawing a deep steadying breath, she allowed herself to look at the check and gasped in shock and surprise. The amount was almost one-third of her entire bring home income for the year! There must be some mistake. The amount couldn't be right. Then she looked at the notes section of the check and a bubble of laughter escaped when she saw that Becky had written—*Yes, it's all yours! Happy Holidays!*—on the memo line.

Digging in her purse, she found a pack of tissues and blew her nose while still gathering her composure; her head swimming at the sudden change in her good fortune. She then opened the paperwork, tears welling again as she looked at the generous partnership contract Ross had had drawn up. But her mind was overwhelmed and she couldn't seem to gather her thoughts enough to take in the details or to even grasp the reality of all the changes that had just taken place in such a short time; it seemed surreal, something she would have to think about another time.

Sighing, she was reaching for the gear shift when she realized the rain had turned to snow. Fat, wet flakes were falling onto the windshield, faster than the wipers could sweep them away. The branches in the trees were starting to grow white and the soft swish of the flakes blanketed her in stillness. Putting the car back in park, she whispered, "Thank you, Father, I feel so undeserving of your blessings. Thank you so much, more than words can say."

Sitting silently, warm and cozy inside the car as the world turned white around her, a peacefulness and contentment settled over her and the joys of the day started to sink in. A smile lit her face and she found she wanted to giggle with happiness. Suddenly eager to share the news, she dug in her purse for the cell phone she still hadn't gotten quite used to carrying, but when she finally found it, she saw that not only was the battery nearly dead, since she had forgotten to charge it, but it was also showing only a weak signal. Ross lived several miles outside of town and the cell service hadn't quite caught up yet. That combined with the weather probably meant she wouldn't have a clear connection even if she was able to place a call. Besides, who would she call first? There were so many people to share the news with.

Dropping the phone back into her bag and putting the car into gear, she gently eased back onto the roadway, surprised to find that the person she was most eager to share the news with was Bob. "I can't wait to tell him," she whispered to herself, imagining his wide smile and assured "I told you so" response. He had been right all along, assuring her of their success and of Ross's approval. He deserved to be told first. Then giving herself a mental shake she thought of her kids. Of course, she couldn't wait to share the news with them and the rest of her family, and Gina of course. Gina would be ecstatic when she hears the news. But mostly, her mind remained with Bob and she couldn't stop her smile of happiness as she thought of his reaction. This had been their shared project, their shared risk…and it had succeeded far better than she had dreamed, and had certainly given a more positive outcome than she could ever have imagined.

December 3

The world must be viewed in shades of gray; it can't be all black or white. And while some things are unforgiveable and no excuse could ever be good enough, others are caused by circumstance. Does a judge know what poverty feels like? Can an upper-middle-class doctor understand why a low income family doesn't come in for routine exams? How can an inner city child relate to kids from upper income families? The fact is, they can't. I guess it all comes back to that old saying, "Don't judge a man until you've walked a mile in his shoes."

So I suppose if I look at my past in shades of gray, I shouldn't blame myself so much for my bad choices. When I married Billy, it seemed like the logical alternative, the obvious decision. No one waved a red rag in my face or even warned me of the drastic step I was taking. But then, we seldom receive notice when we change the course of our lives. And even if anyone had tried to warn me or show me the mistake I was making, I'm sure I wouldn't have listened. I thought I was in love and that's what you do when you're in love, you alter your life, give up your dreams and get married. At least that's how it was then back in the rural area where I grew up. There were very few options after high school, for boys or girls. The coal mines or move away, and few were encouraged to achieve any education beyond high school, at least not those of us that weren't "townies." We were considered little more than white trash, fodder for the coal mines. Children become what they see and if their horizons are never broadened, they will follow the same patterns that are laid before them.

Today, as I drove through one of impoverished "wrong side of the tracks" areas downtown, I stopped for a soda. An attractive teenage girl was showing off the baby on her hip to the clerk. He was about eighteen months old and looked well cared for. He seemed very articulate for his age and she and the clerk laughed as he parroted their words. Her love and pride for him were evident, but my heart ached because I know that right now, right at this moment, she's certain he'll never grow up to be like all the other people in her neighborhood; she is certain that somehow she will find a way for him to be more, achieve more. He will never take drugs or quit school; he will never commit petty crimes or try to find ways to live off of the system. But in that moment as I looked at that baby boy, I knew that if his mommy doesn't do something drastic to give him a better life, something to teach him that there is more to life, to show him that he needs to reach for more, in a few years he will be out there on the street, buying and dealing with his peers.

You become what you see and you accept what you live with daily. The right can become wrong until someone shows you a different world a better way. I can only hope that I have done that—that I have kept my kids from the acceptance of life being just one big party as their dad viewed it; from thinking that it's okay for every occasion to be "celebrated" with a beer. But maybe I have only taught them that constant work yields little reward. I guess only time will tell if I've succeeded.

# End Zones

Dappled autumn sunlight filtered through the branches of the old oak tree that stood at the edge of the deck and bird song filled the air. Tess sipped slowly from the hot cup of coffee that had been heavily laced with mocha creamer, and gathered her robe tighter as she stood in the door way. The day had been graced with sunlight instead of the usual winter's gloom and the sun's rays were gobbling up the remaining patches of white snow, leaving only muddy reminders of yesterday's downpour.

Brushing back the tangled hair from her forehead, she couldn't keep the smile from her face. *This then was the first day of a new beginning*, she thought. Maybe she hadn't screwed up her life as much as she'd thought; maybe she wasn't merely wandering through time, gobbling up days with no chance of arriving at her destination. Perhaps there had been guidance, meaning, and purpose to her choices. Perhaps she hadn't taken all wrong turns after all. But how could one heart hold so much joy without bursting when it all seemed to arrive in just a matter of days?

Her smile widening, she looked again at the letter in her hand that Chad had proudly handed her yesterday when she'd arrived home with her own joyful news. The words in the letter had only made her sense of disorientation grow greater and pushed her heart even closer to the bursting point. The happiness it brought and the words written there had been almost more powerful to her soul than Ross's kind words of thanks. The letter was proof that somehow, even when she hadn't been looking, things had still worked out.

The letter was from Chad's boss and it was filled with words of praise for her son's maturity and his hard work, his commitment. He had quietly been moving Chad's name forward as an entrant into the corporate scholarship funds and the envelope held the first of these—two thousand dollars towards school next fall.

But that wasn't all; he also wanted to enroll Chad in a night class starting in January which the restaurant would pay for. The credits from the class would carry over towards his classes in the fall, and with her permission, he wanted to enter Chad for a full scholarship for a four-year business degree. The letter assured her that even without the full scholarship if Chad chose to, he could complete his degree at the corporation's expense but it might take a little longer. He explained that he felt Chad was district manager material, which to her surprise pulled down a starting salary that was almost equal to what she had earned the previous year, and it came with full benefits.

She couldn't keep the tears from rolling down her face again as she read the words, Chad's future was secured. She held it in her hands. And she'd had very little to do with it; he had found his own way, and Tressa was mapping out her own future as well. Somehow on their own they'd found the answers that had managed to elude her. It made her a little sad, and yet so proud she could hardly contain it. Maybe neither was following the most direct paths or the paths she would have chosen. But maybe this was just another hard part of parenting and certainly the hardest part she'd been faced with yet, and that was being reminded that it was their life after all and at a certain point you had to let go and trust them to find their own way.

Later as she shared a celebratory lunch with Bob and Gina, Tess found her mind racing along on two parallel tracks: one was in the moment, happily clinking her slender fluted champagne glass against Bob and Gina's glasses; and the other was watching Bob as if from a distance, seeing him for the first time for the attractive man that he was. Tall and slender with broad shoulders, dirty blond hair, and soulful brown eyes; he drew attention from women wherever he went. And while he was always friendly, always polite, he seemed immune to the outlandish flirtations some women threw his way. She supposed that came from years of having such advances made towards him. She knew he had dated his fair share, but he was far from the "tomcat" he could have been. He was a hard worker, more interested in the next business venture than the next party; a real catch for some woman some day. She had learned from his mother that he'd been married briefly while still in college. His girlfriend had gotten pregnant and they'd married for the baby's sake. They'd divorced when his daughter was less than a year old and she'd moved with her mother back to her hometown in the San Francisco Bay area. She'd discovered that he saw her a few times a year, although her mom's second husband had adopted her and raised her as his own. Bob had always still contributed to her upbringing and was helping to pay for her education at UC-San Francisco. Apparently, their bond had grown stronger now that she was older and they talked almost daily.

This was a side of him he had kept to himself, but it only made him more attractive to Tess. It showed his tender, softer side. Even the fact that he'd allowed her stepfather to adopt her and raise her as his own showed that he'd cared more for her well being and security than his bragging rights as a father.

She wondered what she had done that life had never allowed her to be loved by a man like that. A tender and caring man, an educated man with class and manners, a gentleman who showed respect to women, a man who would put his family, his home, and his kids first, who would shower his wife with love and affection, not words of anger and belittling. What had she done wrong that a man like that had never given her a second look? True, she was uneducated, but that didn't equal ignorance; she was a hard worker—self taught—she had integrity, grit…but somehow, those men wanted delicate women, ones with a proper degree in the arts or philosophy, a useless degree that they never planned to use since what they'd really majored in was husband hunting. So they never actually worked or used those degrees. Instead, they played homemaker and served on committees and put together charity banquets and passed out reading materials at the hospital.

They were the type of women who knew the right colors to use to decorate a house and the correct wine to go with beef or fish; women who behaved "correctly" at charitable events, dressed in twin sets and pleated capris, not jeans and t-shirts; women who would never, ever dare check the tire pressure or the oil in their Volvos, Audis, Beamers, Explorers, or Town and Country mini vans; women who performed their wifely duties at night, without showing unbecoming excitement or desires or needs of their own; who created cute little code words and nicknames for sex and designated specific nights so their husbands knew which nights they were going to get lucky; who never dreamed of making the first move or displaying spontaneity in their love life. Nope, she wasn't that woman.

Shaking her head, she pushed the thoughts away and returned her attention to the food on her plate. When Gina suddenly jumped from her chair and spiked an imaginary ball, giving a little "end zone" dance, Tess covered her eyes in embarrassment, but couldn't stop the laughter that bubbled up inside of her from escaping.

"We did it! We did it! Whoo-hoo! We did it!" Gina chanted, giving Bob a high five before returning to her seat and impulsively reaching over to give Tess a hug. Tess affectionately hugged the younger woman, happy to share the moment with her. Glancing up she saw Bob watching them and she returned his slow smile. This man had believed in her—her. He hadn't gone to Ross with his proposal, he had come to her. He'd treated her as a full partner, an equal, from the beginning. She might not ever be the love of his life or of any man's life for that matter, but then she'd already determined she wasn't the type of woman a man like Bob would date anyway since she wasn't a "delicate flower," but she could be his business partner, and more than that, she could be his friend. Before she could think the action through, her arm reached out to pull him into a three way hug with her and Gina.

December 4

We can be so focused on what we want the answer to our prayers to be that we often ignore or overlook it when God gives us something different. And while it may not be what we had imagined and while it may lead us in a different direction and challenge us to think beyond what we thought possible, that doesn't mean it isn't a gift, a miracle even, given from God's love. Too often though, because it isn't exactly what we asked for or thought we wanted or thought we should want, we ignore it or wish it away, still clinging to the belief of what we thought we had to have. Sometimes we need to pause and realize that while we are busy wishing for something different, what we have or what we are given is just fine, even preferable, maybe. And that we should love it and appreciate it, or someday we might wake up only fully realizing what we had when it's gone. Long story short: be careful what you wish for!

Earlier, while talking with my daughter and Gina as we sat sipping mochas and nibbling scones at the coffee shop, I felt so content. I felt the love and the struggles of the women who have come before and I felt the pains and disappointments as well as the happiness and joy of the ones who will come after. It upsets me to hear anyone point fingers or blame at the generation that follows, or the one that came before, for we are all human, we all struggle to do the best we can with what we have. Each generation will make mistakes, and each will shape the future, will fulfill dreams and find the best way they can engender to make life the best it can be, not only for themselves, but for those they love. But there will always be the greedy, those that will look only for the money to be made, no matter the cost to others.

As I have said before, we should realize that no thought or idea, no emotion, and no concept is ever totally our own. We are all—each and every one of us—a compilation of those who have come before. We are human, we are man, and we are woman, from 1 to 101. We each can understand the other if we let go of the immature belief that only our generation has ever faced: heartache, failed romances, the urge to break boundaries or set goals, the urge to party and dance, to make love under the stars or to be thought beautiful, to be loved. That only we and those in our generation care about the world, about healthy food, and clean water for our children.

We are all human and we need to throw away our stubbornness and our beliefs that anyone older or younger has nothing to teach us; that they can't understand us or relate to us. Love and understanding, that's all we need… the understanding that we are all human; that we have all been there, that while things change, basic humanity does not. We are either good, or we're not. We are generous or greedy. We care deeply about others, or we care not at all—these are the bases of all of us. What we do with these things and which way we choose to live our lives, those are the choices we must make. And the rest…well, the rest is just window dressing because it's who we are inside that matters.

Tess closed the book, a smile covering her face, a contentment settling into her like a warm, but unfamiliar blanket. Her life was coming together in ways she had certainly never imagined. Her stubbornness made the old visions of what life should be hard to let go of. But the future was here. Things were the way they were. She was raising good children, children with good hearts and good ethics, and maybe those things were more important than cars to drive and the latest clothing styles on their backs. Maybe she'd worried too much about the wrong things.

Picking up her cinnamon hazelnut hot chocolate, she took a long sip and leaned back in the chair. Maybe it was time she relaxed a little, stopped holding on so tight to her anger and frustrations over what things weren't, and just started accepting and cherishing what they were. Perfect? No, but nothing ever was, no matter how it looked from the outside. Even the most perfect family had issues, cracks and fissures at the seams where the imperfections seeped through. Even those who had always lived life by the rules and who'd never colored outside the lines, even they had their own share of failures and disappointments, losses and dissatisfaction. Maybe accepting things just the way they were and realizing that while her life had not been on the conformists' path, it had never been dull; maybe that was the key to contentment.

She felt giddy, excited, and lightheaded almost. How could she have been so self-absorbed with a perceived need to strive for perfection when life was just life? It was hers, hers to enjoy and to savor, to experience, not to agonize over.

Earlier she'd gone shopping with Gina and Tressa, and as she'd struggled to pull her jeans off hopping on one foot in the small dressing room, she'd felt like a clumsy princess, pulling the soft, swirling dresses over her head. She'd felt melancholy that she'd forgotten how it felt to be feminine, to look attractive and "girly" in a swirl of fabric and frills. But when she'd stepped from the dressing room, the look on Gina and Tressa's faces told her she was still a woman.

The dress they all finally agreed on was a knee length shiny slip in a deep, dark sapphire blue, covered in a lacy overlay with tiny threads of silver running through it. The blue made her eyes look dark, like the deep blue of a moonlit night, and the fabric hugged her body like a second skin, the low bodice skimming the tops of her breasts.

In the jeans and tees she usually worn, she'd forgotten she had curves and legs! Legs that seemed long on her short frame, shaped like a dancers with narrow calves and trim ankles. Giddy like a young girl shopping for a prom dress, she'd twirled in front of the mirror, her jaws hurting from the smile that kept bursting forth on her face. And for once, she didn't flinch too much at the price tag but only agreed to take it after Gina reminded her she had a 20 percent off coupon she could use.

They'd completed the outfit with silvery grey hose, a faux fur trimmed black shawl wrap, and the cutest silvery sling backs she'd ever owned; dangling silver earrings that sparkled like a disco ball completed the look, and for the first time in a very long time, she was looking forward to an evening out, not as a mother or as the photographer, but as a guest, as a woman.

December 13

Today, I was remembering my father's last summer. I remember he bought me the bicycle I wanted for Christmas shortly after school started that year. His excuse was that he didn't want to delay things, life was too short. He said Michigan winters were too cold for bike riding. He wanted to see me ride while the weather was still warm. He was kinder to Mom those last few weeks too; allowing her to choose better cuts of meats and her favorite foods from the grocery store, saying the same to her, that life was too short to deny ourselves the best foods except at the holidays. Maybe he had a premonition of his own death, or maybe the fact that mom was now our breadwinner—since he'd gone back to work just long enough to lose his disability before realizing his body could no longer do a hard day's work—had mellowed him; things were different when he was at the mercy of someone else's good will. He was now relegated to cooking and cleaning and keeping an eye on me after school. He'd sold our farm earlier that summer and had already spent most of the money he'd gotten from the sale, leaving just enough for the down payment on the small house where we now lived.

In late April of that same year, Mom, Wesley and I had returned from work and school to the small apartment in Highland Park, Michigan, where we were living then to find the house dark and quiet. We found my dad sitting quietly in the dim living room; a beer can in one hand, a cigarette in the other. He told us he had gone to see a doctor at the Veterans hospital that morning. They had kept him there most of the day, running tests, and at the end of the day, they had told him he had colon cancer and needed to have his colon removed and a colostomy bag attached. Otherwise, the cancer would eventually spread to his other organs and take his life.

He also told us that Grandpa had visited him when he got home that day. Of course, Grandpa had been gone for a year by that time, so if he had visited, it would have to have been in apparition form. But my dad insisted that his father had talked to him. He said he had told him to go back to the mountains and find a particular plant that grew in the forest there. He was supposed to crush the leaves and make tea from it; the tea was supposed to help cure him.

We had been living in Michigan for almost six months by then, but a few weeks later, my parents withdrew me from school early and found a relative for Wes to stay with, and the three of us—my mom, dad and I—went "home" to the mountains for the summer. Becca was finishing her sophomore year in college, but was staying on campus to work for the summer, so the house was quiet with just the three of us.

My mom and I shared one of the big double beds and my dad slept on the couch and the dark, quietness of the country at night seemed scary after the bustling city we had left behind. Cousins and other relatives visited frequently during the day, and we went fishing and on picnics and had a relatively peaceful summer. But to my knowledge, Daddy never looked for the plant he claimed his father had told him to find. Curiously though, the colon cancer was basically ignored when he died. We were told that there were much more serious issues with the cirrhosis of the liver and coal dust coating on his lungs called *black lung* that he also suffered from.

Instead, he remembered where a few more jars of 'shine were hidden and he spent the summer drinking with the friends and family that visited. I've often wished I could remember what the plant was called, but I was just a child and it seemed scary to think of my grandpa visiting in ghost form, so my mind hadn't grasped much of his conversation beyond that.

At the end of July, my dad had sold the farm for far less than what it was worth and we had moved back to Michigan. The small factory where my mother had worked had held her job, and we quickly settled into our new home. After much debate, I was allowed to ride the new purple bicycle to school even though it was several blocks away, and required I cross a four lane street. It wasn't the school we were zoned for, but it was the school I had attended the year before and where my cousins, my Uncle Bill's children attended; my parents hoped it might make it easier for me to not have to start over at a new school.

I didn't tell them that it didn't really change anything. I was still teased and very much a loner. But I loved the long rides to and from school and the independence of riding my bike. I obeyed all street lights and watched for cars; I was very responsible even though I was only in fourth grade. In Michigan at that time, many kids went home for lunch in the middle of the day and then walked back in time for afternoon classes, but I packed my lunch so I only had to make the trip once in the morning and once in the evening and I was always obedient and came straight home after school. Mom had had to switch to evening shift when she'd returned to work, so it was just me and my dad until Wesley came home from work.

Most days he was resting on the sofa when I came home, and I would change my clothes and play outside for awhile before Wesley came home from work. Then the three of us would make dinner together or re-heat the meal my mom had prepared earlier before leaving for work, and then I would settle down to do my homework and get ready for bed. Wes had created a bedroom from the screened in porch added at the back of the house. It was twice as big as any of the actual bedrooms, and sometimes he would let me sit out there with him and his girlfriend while he strummed his guitar.

In late September on an overcast Thursday, I came out of school to find it had been raining even though the air was warm. The patches of leaves made the sidewalk slick and I tried to ride carefully to avoid a fall, but the tires slipped as I came to a stop at the corner of one street. Me, the bike and all my books tumbled sideways. I had tied my windbreaker around my waist, and when I tried to pick the bike up, I found that the dangling sleeves had tangled in the chain. I managed to pull the jacket free from my body but found I couldn't pull it loose from the bike; it was stuck solid, locking the back tire and preventing me from riding.

I could only imagine the trouble I was in. In desperation I pulled and tugged at the chain, the black grease getting onto my hands which I tried to rub clean in the grass, but the jacket stayed firm. I knew my parents would be furious; my jacket sleeve was probably ruined, stained from the grease and possibly torn from the chain, and for all I knew, my new bike was ruined.

    Finally giving up, I resolved myself to the fact that I would have to push the bike home, dragging the back wheel as I walked. It made for a slow trip and I felt foolish as I drug it along, my jacket tangling and dangling along the ground. It made for a long trip and I was several minutes late; the closer I got to the house the slower I walked, fearing my father's wrath, but at last I reached my front yard. I called for my dad, angrily dropping the bike onto the wet grass when he didn't respond. My long, struggling trek had left me tired, thirsty and frustrated, and I would have rather faced his anger at that moment than to delay the inevitable.

    Angrily stomping into the house, I was shocked to find it dark and still: no lights were on, the television was quiet, and the curtains drawn. Pausing in the entryway to give my eyes time to adjust to the gloom, I at last spotted my father on the sofa; he was asleep, his hands folded on his chest, lying perfectly still, as if already posed for his coffin.

    Sighing, I reached down to remove my sneakers and tiptoed through the darkened room to the bathroom, which was in the center of the even darker hallway. Entering the bathroom to wash my hands, I grabbed for the sink as my foot slipped in something wet and slimy. I remember wondering what I had done to deserve such a messed up day as I reached for the light switch. The brightness was startling and I blinked several times, unsure if my eyes were actually seeing what I thought they were.

    As the reality hit me that yes, it was blood, and yes, I had stepped into the center of the pile of mucous filled blood. I gagged and stifled back a scream as I ripped the sock from my foot, dropping it into the center of the bloody mess on the floor; it's whiteness a sharp contrast to the bright, glistening of the partially congealed blood. The pool seemed dark, black almost, except for where my foot had disturbed it. There it was a bright red and it filled me with horror and I trembled from head to toe as I looked at it. Then the smell reached me, a thick, heavy metallic smell that seemed to get stuck in my throat and nose, like the smells on butchering day back on the farm.

Backing quickly from the room I ran back out the front door shaking from head to toe, gulping in the cool fall air as I fought down the bile that rose in my throat, gagging and coughing until I calmed enough to sit down on the stoop, shivering as I waited for Wes to get home, unaware that I still wore no shoes and only one sock.

Wes must've cleaned up the mess, I can't remember. I only remember him making me a cup of hot chocolate milk and settling me in the center of my mom's bed. I must've fallen asleep because when I awoke much, much later, I had a blanket over me. I could hear Wes and my mom as they pleaded with my dad to go to the hospital, and the weakness and tiredness of his replies as he refused. Afraid to move, imaging the horror of stumbling into another pile of blood, I snuggled quietly under the blanket and fell back to sleep.

The next thing I knew, my mom was waking me up for school. We quietly went about the morning routine with no mention of the horror from the evening before, but as I was leaving, she followed me out the door to my bike, which Wes had also repaired the night before. Giving me a hug, she handed me an envelope.

"I don't want you to go to school today," she told me. "I'm not going to work either. I need you to help me with getting your dad to a doctor so I want you to ride to your Uncle Bill's house and give him this note. Then I want you to just stay with your aunt, and Mommy will come and get you later after Uncle Bill and I take care of Daddy. I want him to come and help me convince your dad to go to the hospital. He won't listen to me and Wes, but I think he'll listen to Bill."

I felt important, included, being used as a carrier pigeon, carrying the note to my Uncle's house; we didn't have a telephone. Telephones cost money, and my parents had decided to delay getting one until they saw what the typical monthly utilities were in the new house. I remember my mom smoothing my hair before she kissed my cheek, sensing the fear and anxiety that raced through my body after what I had witnessed the night before. "It'll be okay. Your daddy's just been drinking too much again." She reassured me.

I looked down at the ground, rubbing my sneaker against the wet grass. "Is that why there was blood?" I asked quietly.

She nodded. "Yes, honey, Daddy said he was throwing up blood." She watched my face for my reaction, and when at last I looked up at her, she smiled. "I love you, baby girl, and I need you to be careful and get to Uncle Bill's house quickly to let him know I need him. Mommy is counting on you."

Nodding, I reached out to hug her in return and then climbing onto my bike, I pushed off to begin my ride.

My Uncle, my dad's younger brother, lived several blocks beyond my school, but I knew the way well. I frequently rode to their house to play with my cousins, so I wasn't scared or bothered by the longer ride. Nor did the idea of my dad going to the hospital bother me very much. He'd been hospitalized so much during my lifetime already that it seemed almost routine. But the blood, the shock of having stepped in it, that did bother me; apparently, even more than I realized at the time since I buried that memory for many, many years.

Maybe part of the memory repression was because—little did I know, as I rode away from our house on that rainy, cool September morning—I would never see my father alive again.

# Delphinium Blue

Hair curled, make-up perfect, new dress, heels, and jewelry, all in place. *Time to go*, Tess thought, nervously wiping her palms along the sides of the dress. She felt a little melancholy, in spite of her pleasure at being all dressed up. Shouldn't being dressed up result in the hope that someone special might notice? Shouldn't someone special be coming to pick her up soon, the doorbell ringing, nerves jangling? Shaking her head, she scolded herself; that was for a much younger woman, one whose hopes and dreams of a family hadn't come true yet. "Been there, done that," she reminded herself. Pasting a happy smile on her face, she went to find Tressa to get a second opinion.

The kids all clapped when she entered the living room, and she gave a small twirl, laughing as they jumped up, all chattering at once. Their excitement at seeing her dressed up made her heart soar. Soon, her little goslings would leave the nest and like Old Mother Hubbard, she'd have to get a dog; a big old yellow dog that was clumsy and lovable. Either that or maybe she could turn into the Crazy Cat Woman and have sixteen cats.

"You guys are all set for the evening, right? And of course, you know how to reach me if you need me. I'll probably not stay too long; I don't want you here alone too late. Make sure Sammy brushes his teeth and…"

"Mom, mom…hey mom!" Chad clapped his hands and gently grasped her shoulders until she stopped chattering. "We'll be fine; we're big kids now, except for the pipsqueak of course." Chad grinned at his younger brother.

Sammy piped out an indignant, "Hey," of protest and threw a punch at his much bigger brother, making them all laugh.

Chad wrestled his little brother into stillness, pinning his arms behind his back. "My point is that we'll be fine, Mom! We have food, a warm house, movies to watch, we're all good," Chad finished, shaking Sammy's arms as he added, "And we promise not to search the house for unwrapped Christmas presents; right, Sam?"

Tess couldn't help but laugh again when Sam nodded his head in agreement, then with a giggle, proudly displayed the crossed fingers of both hands. Smiling, she reached out to give her oldest son a warm hug. "Thanks sweetheart, you're a good son."

"Please, Mom. Please go and have a wonderful time." Tressa gave her a hug as well. "You look wonderful and it's been so long since you've had an evening out. Please, have a good time, for all of us. When you come home, you can tell us all about how beautiful Becky has the house decorated and all the great food, the lights, everything. Just relax and go have a great time, okay?" Tressa's pleading and sweet words were a warm balm and made it easy to overlook the unwashed loads of laundry straining against the folding doors of the laundry area, or the dirty dishes and trash the kids had already accumulated in the living room with their drinks and snacks.

She kissed Tressa's cheek just as the doorbell rang. "Oh, that'll be Grant and Patty; they're giving me a ride." She moved to open the door, but with a gentle push Tressa moved past her.

"Here, you stand right here." Tressa moved her gently back around the corner, into the hallway. "Don't come into the living room until I call you."

"But it's just Grant and Patty." Tess protested.

"Mom, come on, just this once, make an entrance!" Tressa smiled at her. "Please?"

Acquiescing, she nodded her head and stayed where she'd been placed while she nervously waited for Tressa to go to the door.

"Wow, don't you look nice!" She heard her daughter exclaim, feeling the rush of cool December air swirl around her feet and legs from the open door. "Oooh, that's beautiful!" She heard her daughter exclaim. "Wait right here, I'll get her."

Tess had just started to move into the living room when Tressa rounded the corner so suddenly that they almost collided. "Mom, mom, please don't be mad," Tressa was whispering quickly. "He asked me mom, he asked me and I told him it would be a great surprise. Remember that Mom, he asked; he wanted to do this. Okay? And yum, you smell great, by the way." She buzzed her mom's cheek. "So just have a good time, and please...please don't be upset with me."

Her heart raced as her daughter's words sank in...but she was being gently propelled forward and there was no time to question, no time to protest. Turning the corner, she met Bob's gaze and a small gasp escaped her lips as she took in how totally masculine he looked. Like a *GQ* model; he looked absolutely picture perfect. He was dressed in a sharp deep charcoal grey pinstripe suit, his shirt was a grayish blue and he had a small blue boutonniere pinned to his lapel. Time seemed to stop as she realized he was drinking her in as completely as she was checking him out, from toes to hair. And then their eyes met and a slow smile lit up his face. A warmth spread through her as she returned the smile and her heart seemed to skip a beat.

Stepping forward, he held out the corsage box he'd been holding and she smiled as she looked down at the beautiful wrist corsage it held. It was a perfect match for his boutonniere, a perfect match for her outfit. The tiny flowers and even the ribbon were blue, delphinium flowers – delphinium blue, the color of the brightest sky and the most peaceful sea; associated with depth and stability, trust, intelligence, and faith.

Suddenly, she realized what Tressa's words had meant; her cunning daughter had agreed to this behind her back, even giving him the color of her dress so he could coordinate the corsage. A flash of irritation flashed over her, but then, as he gently pulled the corsage onto her wrist, the anger melted and she turned to smile at her daughter, who giggled in relief at her mother's beaming face.

Reaching back, she hugged her daughter, whispering into her ear, "This is what I get for letting you two work together so much!" Tressa giggled again and returned the hug. "You know I ought to ground you!"

"But you won't!" Tressa smiled and reached out to help her with her wrap. "I want you to be happy, to have a magical night. Okay? And tomorrow, I want to hear all about it." She kissed her mom's cheek and stepped back, watching as her mom blew kisses to the boys and then turned one last time to wink at her. Tressa giggled again, seeing her mom's smile made happiness wash over her.

Bob held the door, turning to smile and mouth the word "thanks" to Tressa as he closed it tight behind them. As they stepped down from the small stoop, Tess noticed he wasn't driving his usual beat-up old Chevy Tahoe, but instead, a sharp, shiny, deep blue Cadillac Crossover SUV sat in the driveway. She paused, turning an inquisitive eye to him. He grinned sheepishly before rushing ahead to open the door for her.

"It's kind of a test drive. I thought maybe it was time I drove something that looked a little more successful than that beat-up old Tahoe. I told them I had a special date tonight, so…they let me bring it home for the weekend."

She didn't miss his use of the word date, but decided not to give it too much power or she'd get nervous. "Dark blue?" She asked. His Tahoe was black and he'd once made a comment that he usually only bought cars in silver or black.

He shrugged, "It's my new favorite color." His eyes were intense as he watched her and she smiled shyly, her mind turning, wondering if Tressa had told him blue was her favorite color as she settled herself into the soft leather seat of the new car.

"And? How do you like it so far?" she asked, rubbing the padded leather of the dash with her hands.

He slowly returned her smile and said, "I think I just might keep it," before softly closing the door.

His words seemed to have a double meaning and she couldn't stop smiling as she snuggled into the warmth of the heated seat. Thankful for Bob's thoughtfulness to have turned it on before coming to the door as the warmth spread through her like melted chocolate, soothing her jangled nerves.

It was time to relax, to just be who she was. It was enough for him when they were working together in business. There, he accepted her for whom and what she was. They were friends, business partners; she didn't need to be nervous, and it wasn't like a blind date with someone she didn't know. So maybe it was time to stop thinking about their differences, about the huge socioeconomic chasm that divided them, and instead think of their sameness. Of the work ethics they shared, the love of a challenge, the love of business. She could accept it for what it was, even if it turned out to be nothing more than just a fun evening with her business partner and friend.

And maybe she needed to do this because maybe, just maybe, she'd been wrong, about so many things. But most of all, because maybe, just maybe, an educated man like Bob could see himself with someone like her after all.

DUPLICATE
PROGRESS RECORD

FINAL SUMMARY

Date of Admission:   9/25/19??
Date of Expiration:  9/30/19??

This 47 year old male was admitted on 9/25/19?? with a history of chronic and acute alcohol intake over the past 10 – 15 years. One day prior to his admission after a heavy drinking spree he had hematemesis and melena. He also had a past history of perforated ulcer.

On admission his lungs were clear; his heart rate was normal; there was a normal sinus rhythm, no murmur was heard. The liver was two fingerbreadths below the right costal margin and tender. Rectal examination was normal. Patient had coarse flapping tremors.

He was seen also by Dr. Vander.

On admission his serum electrolytes were normal. Amylase and lipase were within normal limits. Hemoglobin 10.5 gm. Gonadotropes 31. Repeat hemoglobin dropped to 9.4. His glucose was 80. Stools on two occasions were negative for occult blood. Serum potassium repeated was 4.3; BUN 8; BSP was 1; SCOT and LDH were normal. Alkaline phosphatase was normal Bilirubin was normal. VDRL was non-reactive.

Patient was given two units of blood. His hemoglobin rose to 12.2. Serum magnesium was normal. Repeat serum-electorlytes on 9/27 were normal. His electrocardiogram showed sinus tachycardia, no other abnormalities. Patient's chest x-ray showed a fractured clavicle.

Patient was given Librium, Tigan, Maalox, Ringer's Lactate, and further I.V. fluid with potassium chloride and was also given Sparine and later was given Magnesium Sulphate. His intake and output was adequate. His temperature ranged from 99 to 100. He was restless and twitching throughout his hospital stay. He had no apparent reaction from his transfusion. He was grossly disoriented throughout his hospital stay and was incontinent. He continued to cough up thick mucus. He began sweating profusely and expired at 5:50 A.M. on 9/30/19??.

Autopsy was performed but the results are not available at this time.